Narrative Inquiries from Fulbright Lecturers in China

This collection of nine Fulbright educators' narrative accounts examines how these scholars navigated their teaching responsibilities with students, time with fellow colleagues, and cultural expectations in China, ranging from experience in teaching arts and government to questions of religion, emotional literacy, and urban infrastructure. With these contributions, authors analyze their own expectations against their actual experiences in order to offer insights for scholars and students of study abroad programming. As a roadmap for negotiating China's higher education network and for taking advantage of any cross-cultural educational environment, this book highlights the type of fruitful educational programming that can come from cultural, historical, economic, and political difference.

Shin Freedman is Head of Scholarly Resources & Collections of Whittemore Library at Framingham State University and teaches Communication Arts courses through Framingham State University's Division of Graduate and Continuing Education, US.

Pat Munday is Professor of Science and Technology Studies at Montana Tech, USA.

Jeannette W. Cockroft is Associate Professor of History and Political Science at Schreiner University, USA, and Chair of the Department of History and Regional Studies.

Narrative Inquiries from Fulbright Lecturers in China

Cross-Cultural Connections in Higher Education

Edited by Shin Freedman, Pat Munday, and Jeannette W. Cockroft

Routledge
Taylor & Francis Group

LONDON AND NEW YORK

First published 2019
by Routledge
2 Park Square, Milton Park, Abingdon, Oxon OX14 4RN
605 Third Avenue, New York, NY 10017

First issued in paperback 2020

Routledge is an imprint of the Taylor & Francis Group, an informa business

Library of Congress Cataloguing-in-Publication Data
A catalog record for this book has been requested

ISBN 13: 978-0-367-72768-0 (pbk)
ISBN 13: 978-1-138-32083-3 (hbk)

Typeset in Times New Roman
by Apex CoVantage, LLC

Contents

Preface

The story of how this book came to be provides a first glimpse into the context, challenges, and opportunities surrounding US Fulbright scholars in China. Hardly a day goes by these days without geopolitical news about China and the US, whether it's Chinese student visa issues, tariffs, and a looming trade war or China's connection with North Korea. These issues seem more prominent since the 2016 US election.

Narrative Inquiries from Fulbright Lecturers in China: Cross-Cultural Connections in Higher Education features nine Fulbright scholars writing about their experiences as scholars in China. Grounded by the narrative inquiry framework and data from memories, artifacts, WeChat (China's Facebook-like social media platform), and lived experiences, they retell stories, truths, voices, interpretations, and reflections based on their 2016–2017 academic year. The book also includes a chapter from an early US-China Fulbright scholar, who was in China in 1980 and whose historical experience will be of interest to both teachers and researchers contemplating work in China.

While traveling on the US-China Fulbright university lecture circuit in the late fall of 2016, this author visited Southwest University in Chongqing, where one of my co-editors was teaching. We compared notes on our Fulbright experience—teaching, lecturing, and campus lives—and realized the differences and commonalities of our experiences. Her *waiban* (the university liaison who works with foreign guests) regularly met with her and seemed deeply concerned about her experience at the university, whereas this author rarely saw her *waiban* for any reason. Only when this author shared the remembrance of her friend's experience as a Fulbright scholar in China, after China had just opened up to the world thirty-eight years ago, did we realize that our current insights may be of value to other scholars who might visit China, and thus we became convinced that our Fulbright stories were worth sharing.

Over the next few weeks, this author began to wonder whether other Fulbrighters had had similar experiences that others could learn from. What if my cohorts and I wrote about our experiences and published them as collected essays in a book format? Could we capture and share our experiences with potential Fulbrighters, other scholars contemplating work in China, higher education administrators in the US and China, and a wider group of general readers? Hence the idea of this book was born.

Initially, we considered the publication arm of the Fulbright Commission as a publisher for this book. That idea was quickly abandoned after inquiries to our immediate network, including the education and cultural attaché at the US Embassy in Beijing and the Fulbright Program staff at the Council for International Exchange of Scholars. Instead, finding an academic press publisher and getting a contract signed for the book proposal turned out to be a bigger and more arduous task than I had anticipated. This author shopped the proposal to several university presses at universities with many Fulbright scholar awards. To my surprise, the editors I approached were not interested in publishing the book. Finally, it was Routledge Publishing that expressed support for the book proposal and recommended the use of the narrative inquiry framework as a methodology for describing Fulbright experiences in China. Ironically, after signing the book contract with Routledge, the US-China Fulbright Program staff in Beijing expressed an interest and offered funding to support the book project. This gracious offer, though received with gratitude, was respectfully declined in order to ensure the independence of the collected essays in this volume.

This author deeply appreciates the effort of my colleagues and Fulbright cohorts who participated in previous conversations to test and discuss the groundwork for the book and who ultimately contributed essays for the book proposal. The contributors to this volume, except one, were Fulbright scholars from the 2016–2017 academic-year cohort in China and represented diverse disciplines: library and information science, American history and politics, philosophy, architecture, arts, journalism, educational psychology, teaching English as a second language, and public health. They all had been to China before as college lecturers, business consultants, teachers of English language learners, and above all as adventurous travelers. As these contributors came from geographically diverse parts of the US, from Texas to the Midwest and from New England to Montana, so were their connections to the Chinese teaching communities similarly diverse, ranging from Guangzhou to Changchun to Ningxia to Beijing.

This book makes a distinctive and important contribution to the literature of global education and research, China studies, cultural and global politics, and teaching and learning in China. It is a must read for three groups: teaching and research faculty in all stages of their careers (early-career, mid-career, and senior-level) who plan to teach and/or conduct research in China; aspiring young college, graduate, or PhD students who have an interest in the culture, geopolitics, and educational perspectives in China; and Chinese students, educators, and administrators in the Chinese higher education system who are involved with foreign scholars in China.

Shin Freedman
Boston, January 2019

Acknowledgments

Thank you to Nathan Keltner, formerly with the Fulbright office in Beijing, for suggestions on bureaucratic terminology and advice on some sensitive issues.

Fulbright China Map

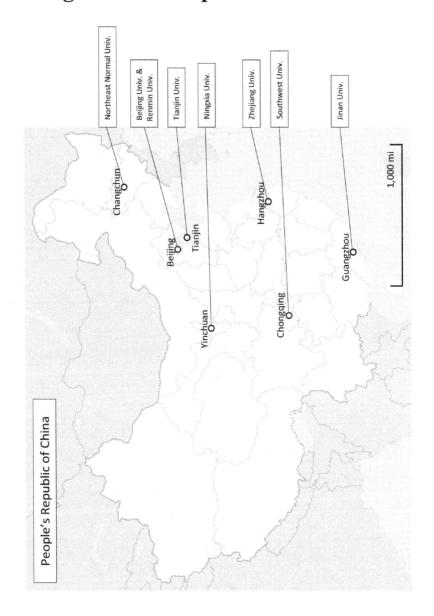

1   Introduction

Shin Freedman, Pat Munday, and Jeannette W. Cockroft

Water is fluid, soft, and yielding. But water will wear away rock, which is rigid and cannot yield. As a rule, whatever is fluid, soft, and yielding will overcome whatever is rigid and hard. This is another paradox: what is soft is strong.

—Lao Tzu

Cross the river by feeling for stones under one's feet.

—Deng Xiaoping

A Brief History of the US-China Fulbright Program

The 2016–2017 academic year marked the seventieth anniversary of the Fulbright Program, the United States' preeminent program for international scholarly exchange. Although the history of Sino-American academic exchange predates the Fulbright Program, the history of that exchange reflects the enduring and sometimes tempestuous nature of the Sino-American relationship.

As part of a larger American commitment to the creation of a liberal democratic framework within which to reconstruct the post–World War II world, President Harry S Truman signed the Fulbright Act on August 1, 1946. Named for its sponsor, Democratic Senator J. William Fulbright of Arkansas, the bill reflected Fulbright's own belief in the value of international educational exchange and the potential of cross-cultural communication to promote world peace and understanding.[1]

A series of bilateral agreements were signed between the United States and the Republic of China on November 10, 1947, with the academic exchange to begin August 1948. China was the first country to participate in the Fulbright Program, and Derk Bodde of the University of Pennsylvania was the first Fulbright scholar. In the twenty months of the program from August 1948 to August 1949, twenty-seven American visiting professors, research fellows, and graduate students traveled to China, while twenty-four Chinese scholars traveled to the United States.[2]

However, by August 1949, the Fulbright Program in China was over. Massive inflation, infrastructure collapse, and the impending victory of the Chinese Communists crippled both the Nationalist Chinese and American efforts to administer the program. After American refusal to recognize the newly established People's Republic of China, Sino-American cultural exchange did not resume until the normalization of diplomatic relations in 1979.

The US-China Fulbright Program during the 1980s focused on teacher training, instruction in English as a second language, and the acquisition of scientific and technical expertise. Scholars in these fields taught at four institutions in Beijing, Shanghai, and Tianjin.[3] This emphasis reflected the Chinese government's prioritization of technological modernization and English language mastery as the cornerstones of its opening to the West. In 1983, the American Lecturer and Chinese Researcher Programs were broadened to include American Studies, defined by the Chinese government to include disciplines such as history, political science, literature, and philosophy.[4] From 1980–1989, twenty-four Fulbright scholars traveled annually to China, and twenty-four Chinese scholars traveled annually to the US.[5]

The Chinese government suspended the 1989–1990 academic exchange to protest American objections to the military crackdown on student protesters in Tiananmen Square. In 1991, the Fulbright Program resumed on a much smaller scale. In 2004, the governments of the United States and China signed an agreement both to expand the program and to fund it more equitably. The number of Chinese institutions involved has increased from forty-one to one hundred twenty-five. Since 1979, over three thousand Chinese and American scholars, lecturers, and graduate students have participated in the Fulbright Program.[6]

To commemorate the seventieth anniversary of the Fulbright Program, we dedicate this collection of essays. With one exception—an early Fulbrighter who was in China during 1980–1982—the contributors to this collection were in China during one or both of the 2016–2017 academic-year semesters.

Narrative Inquiry as a Research Methodology

The authors employ narrative inquiry as a research methodology for storytelling. Sometimes called narrative analysis, this methodology originated in management science as a qualitative approach to better understand how organizations function, solve problems, and make decisions. By the late 1980s, narrative inquiry was taken up by the humanities and social sciences as part of what became known as "the narrative turn."[7] It is a broad and flexible approach and often employs a conventional temporal or synchronic narrative structure with a beginning that addresses the who/what/when/where questions, a middle with some sort of problem or complication that may progress to a climax, and an end resolution or conclusion.[8]

Data collection may consist of formal processes, such as interviews and participant observation. Data collection and analysis may also proceed less informally through collaboration or other interactions or, as Clandinin and Connelly describe it, "collaboration between researcher and participants, over time, in a place or series of places, and in social interaction with milieus."[9] An excellent example of this sort of collaboration or interaction in narrative inquiry is the story of Ming Fang He. Clandinin and Connelly provide a brief narrative overview of her collaboration with Michael Connelly, and she employed narrative inquiry in her own book and several articles about the development of transnational identity for scholars.[10]

Clandinin and Huber wrote, "Three commonplaces of narrative inquiry, temporality, sociality, and place, specify dimensions of an inquiry and serve as a conceptual framework."[11] Temporality evokes the phenomenological sense of being in the moment, drawing on Heraclitus's principle that you can't step in the same river twice because both you and the river change over time. Sociality, or social milieu, involves the personal dimensions of research; as Clandinin and Rosiek explain, "we mean the feelings, hopes, desires, aesthetic reactions and moral dispositions" of the researchers and their subjects.[12] Place considers the geographical context or "sense of place," as the concept came to be known in the 1970s.[13] Yi-Fu Tuan's geography of communication is instructive in this regard, especially in the way that people create narratives that connect personal identity with place, and Paul C. Adams has further built on Tuan's work.[14]

As a form of analysis, special emphasis is placed on the roles of the researcher and actors as the story unfolds, in terms of how the various actors embody the key themes and the ways that the researcher and actors change through time.[15] For the analysis of character development,

> Chase (2005) identified five diverse approaches for analyzing told stories: a psychosocial developmental approach; an identity approach with a focus on how people construct themselves within institutional, cultural, and discursive contexts; a sociological approach with a focus on specific aspects of people's lives; a narrative ethnographic approach and an autoethnographic approach.[16]

Polkinghorne combined Merleau-Ponty's phenomenology and Levi-Strauss's approach to mythology to focus on character development as a way to "transform the passing of life into an adventure of significance and drama."[17]

Several other features of narrative inquiry bear mention. One is the notion of narrative smoothing, whereby a researcher might sacrifice irrelevant events to aid the construction of a coherent narrative.[18] The researcher may also combine several events into a single one or create composite characters.[19] The latter technique is adapted from journalism, and Hollowell asserted, "At its best, composite characterization allows the journalist to compress documented evidence from a variety of sources into a vivid and unified telling of the story."[20]

Narrative methodology, as a unifying approach, provided Fulbrighters diverse ways to discuss their interactions with students and colleagues and their interactions with culture and place. The nine chapters in this book reflect the wide range of academic fields and particular experiences of Fulbright scholars in China. The contributions to this volume are as varied as the authors and their host universities. China is a large country, about the same size as the United States. The geographic diversity of the two nations is comparable, but the cultural diversity of China is much greater than that of the United States when it comes to the sheer number of recognized minorities. Although the Han ethnic group constitutes a 92% majority, there are fifty-five additional recognized ethnic minorities. Even within Han people, there are major differences between northern and southern regions and eastern and western regions. The situation is reflected by language diversity, with distinct regional dialects and some fundamentally different languages. The map of China, with its shape often referred to as "the chicken" by Chinese citizens, preceding this introduction shows the specific locations for the nine Fulbrighters represented in this collection.

Summary of the Chapters

Following this introduction and the map, the book opens with a historical memoir by Tim Maciel about his experience in 1980 to 1982. The US-China Fulbright Program had just been revived after the long Cold War-driven hiatus that began in 1949 and ended with the normalization of diplomatic relations in 1979. For foreign scholars who have worked in China after Deng Xiaoping's economic reforms took hold in the 1990s, the Chinese university Maciel describes in the coastal northeast city of Tianjin would be unrecognizable. His experience was further heightened by the aftermath of a major earthquake that had leveled much of the region in 1976 and by the anti-Western rhetoric that had prevailed during the Cultural Revolution of the late 1960s and early 1970s. Despite challenges ranging from administrators practicing the Chinese cultural style of indirect communication to his students' deeply ingrained misconceptions about American culture, Maciel exemplified the "flow like water" coping mechanism that characterizes the ideal foreign scholar. Also, as a deep lesson that touches many foreign scholars in China and fulfills Senator J. William Fulbright's vision that we should understand how other people live and appreciate the problems they face, Maciel succeeded in building the "guanxi" (关系) that is a cornerstone of Chinese culture and ultimately crucial to the ongoing success of the US-China Fulbright Program.

The next four chapters, by Jesse Butler, Shin Freedman, Pat Munday, and Amy Cheng, move us into the 2016–2017 foreign scholar experience. They exemplify various aspects of academic culture at Chinese universities and provide cautionary tales about essentialism, or over-generalizing one's experience at a single Chinese university to all Chinese universities. Butler uses narrative inquiry to investigate the philosophy of identity in a course he taught on self-knowledge at Jinan University in the southeastern city of Guangzhou. In class essays that encouraged students to explore the notion of identity and how this might be culturally determined, students displayed an impressive knowledge of American culture unknown to Maciel's students in the early 1980s. Also, in an observation shared by many foreign teachers in China, the students were close and attentive readers of sources such as Benjamin Franklin and Ralph Waldo Emerson that our American students often find tedious. Freedman taught Information Literacy and Research Strategies at Zhejiang University in Hangzhou on the east coast. Like many foreign scholars in China, she had to cope with challenges, such as substandard housing and a less-than-supportive university administration. Being a Fulbrighter, Freedman embraced the "flow like water" mantra and worked her way through such challenges using a combination of gentle-but-insistent diplomacy, self-reliance, and support from the US-China Fulbright staff in Beijing. By the end of her stay, she was grateful and impressed by her students' diligence and learning, and she had bonded with her Chinese language tutor, who, in a rare act of Chinese hospitality, invited Freedman into her home for a holiday dinner. Munday taught at Ningxia University in a northwestern province with a large Hui Muslim population, an area seldom visited by Westerners. His classes became a segue for conversations and—for Munday—learning what it meant to be a minority Hui Muslim in a nation overwhelmingly dominated by Han Chinese culture. Through weekly dinners with students and tours into the remote mountainous countryside, he expanded this understanding of Chinese diversity through history, geography, and local culture. Cheng, in her chapter about teaching painting at Renmin University in Beijing, found an art culture gap not easily reconciled. Because of the closure of China to the West and close alliances with Russia from 1946 to the 1970s, Renmin developed a style of art education that emphasizes teaching over practice. For example, Renmin art students tend to learn modernist principles, such as the Bauhaus movement, through lectures and not through studio education. This has led to what Cheng calls "space-related visual illiteracy." By the middle of her Fulbright experience, however, Cheng had learned to teach "seeing" by modeling art critique—guiding students through a gallery and performing formal analysis to explain how a painting uses line, shape, form, space, and so on to achieve particular visual and aesthetic effects.

The next two chapters, by Jeannette W. Cockroft and Mary Ni, demonstrate ways that foreign scholars can connect with students and colleagues at a meaningful extracurricular level. Cockroft, who taught American government at Southwest University in Chongqing, found that her teaching and essay assignments on topics such as democracy and "design your own government" stimulated her students' curiosity about American culture and led to after-class discussions ranging from Christianity to feminism. Activities such as creating "English corners" (informal gatherings for practicing English) and sightseeing tours with students facilitated these conversations. Ni taught a peer counseling/emotional literacy paradigm at Northeast Normal University in the northeastern industrial city of Changchun. As an example of identity development through narrative inquiry, this was a way of confronting her own minority experience as a Chinese-American. Teaching one graduate-level class and developing a series of workshops and lectures, she sought out additional opportunities to interact with her Chinese hosts through a Chinese-English language exchange at a local coffeehouse. Her chapter epitomizes her motto, "We teach what we want to learn," and her experience now reverberates through her daily WeChat (a Facebook-like social media platform ubiquitous in China) communications and newfound sense of confidence as a Chinese-American scholar.

The final two chapters in this collection, by Michael Fetters and Jonathan Ochshorn, engage with some of the bigger-picture issues that arise with foreign scholars navigating life in China. Fetters held a Fulbright Distinguished Chair with Peking University Health Sciences Center. His chapter includes anecdotes about his consternation with the trash dump in the courtyard of his apartment building, ways of coping with various kinds of air pollution, and working through his anxiety when visited by two agents from the National Security Office. Ochshorn taught architecture at Tianjin University near Beijing. Although largely about residential buildings and transportation infrastructure in Tianjin, his chapter is representative of the massive changes (with mixed results) that have taken place in China in recent decades. In the classroom, Ochshorn provides a good foreign teacher lesson in how he dealt with having been assigned a class for foreign (non-Chinese) students that did not meet with US-China Fulbright guidelines.

How to Use This Book

The key to understanding and appreciating this book is simple. Readers may sample the cross-cultural differences of each location where the Fulbright educators resided in the order the chapters are presented, or readers may read the chapters in any order, as each story stands by itself. Regardless of where and how they start the book, readers may learn the sense of what it feels like to teach and live as a foreign expert in China, as Fulbright scholars are referred to, and learn strategies to deal with challenges in and out of the classroom. More importantly, readers will glean new knowledge about the experience of foreign scholars in China from each educator's reflections.

What Makes This Book Special?

This book makes a distinctive and important contribution to the literature of global education and research, China studies, cultural and global politics, and teaching and learning in China. The book will benefit many types of readers, including (1) teaching or research faculty in all stages of their career (early-career, mid-career, and senior-level) who plan to teach and/or conduct research in China; (2) college graduates or those in PhD programs who have an interest in the culture, geopolitics, and educational perspectives in China; (3) Chinese students, educators, and administrators in the Chinese higher education system in China who are involved with foreign scholars; and (4) general readers in the US and elsewhere who are interested in modern China. The audience may also include parents with college-age children or others who might be interested in the experience of living and working in China. Also, higher education administrators who advocate for global or international education and who support professional growth and development of faculty will benefit from reading this book.

Without further ado, let's explore the first chapter.

Notes

1. Walter Johnson and Francis J. Colligan, *The Fulbright Program: A History* (Chicago: University of Chicago Press, 1965), 13.
2. "History," accessed December 4, 2018, https://china.usembassy-china.org.cn/education-culture/academic-exchange/fulbright-program/.
3. Ibid.
4. Ibid.
5. Associated Press, "China Will Resume Fulbright Program," *Los Angeles Times*, March 6, 1990. Web. December 2, 2018.
6. *2012–2013 Fulbright China Directory*, provided by Beijing American Center, cited by Fu Meirong and Xin Zhao, "Utilizing the Effects of the Fulbright Program in Contemporary China: Motivational Elements in Chinese Scholars'

Post-Fulbright Life," *Cambridge Journal of China Studies* 12, nos. 2–3 (2017): 2. Print.

7. Ronald J. Berger and Richard Quinney, eds., *Storytelling Sociology: Narrative as Social Inquiry* (Boulder, CO: Lynne Rienner Publishers, 2005). Print.

8. Catherine Kohler Riessman, *Narrative Analysis: Qualitative Research Methods Series 30* (Newbury Park: Sage Publications, 1993). Print.

9. D. Jean Clandinin and F. Michael Connelly, *Narrative Inquiry: Experience and Story in Qualitative Research* (San Francisco: Jossey-Bass, 2000), 20. Print.

10. Ibid., 51–54; Ming Fang He, "A Narrative Inquiry of Cross-Cultural Lives: Lives in Canada," *Journal of Curriculum Studies* 34, no. 3 (2002): 323–342 and *A River Forever Flowing: Cross-Cultural Lives and Identities in the Multicultural Landscape* (Charlotte, NC: Information Age Publishing, 2000). Print.

11. D. Jean Clandinin and Janice Huber, "Narrative Inquiry," in *International Encyclopedia of Education*, 3rd ed., ed. Barry McGaw, Eva Baker, and Penelope Peterson (New York City: Elsevier, In Press), 3. Web. 01 April 2018.

12. D. Jean Clandinin and Jerry Rosiek, "Mapping a Landscape of Narrative Inquiry: Borderland Spaces and Tensions," in *Handbook of Narrative Inquiry: Mapping a Methodology*, ed. D. Jean Clandinin (Thousand Oaks, CA: Sage Publication, 2007), 69. Print.

13. René Jules Dubos, *The Genius of the Place*, vol. 10 (University of California, School of Forestry and Conservation, 1970), and Sharon Paquin-Staple, "Songs for Gaia: Gary Snyder's Sense of Place" (PhD diss., California State University, Chico, 1982). Print.

14. Clandinin and Rosiek, 69.

15. Jerome S. Bruner, *Actual Minds, Possible Worlds* (Cambridge, MA: Harvard University Press, 1985); Donald E. Polkinghorne, "Narrative Configuration in Qualitative Analysis," *International Journal of Qualitative Studies in Education* 8, no. 1 (1995): 5–23. Print.

16. Clandinin and Huber, 6. They are referring to Susan E. Chase, "Narrative Inquiry: Multiple Lenses, Approaches, Voices," in *The Sage Handbook of Qualitative Research*, 3rd ed., ed. Norman K. Denzin and Yvonna S. Lincoln (Thousand Oaks, CA: Sage Publications, 2005), 651–679. Print.

17. Donald E. Polkinghorne, *Narrative Knowing and the Human Sciences* (Albany, NY: State University of New York Press, 1998), 31, cf. 82–83. Print.

18. Donald P. Spence, "Narrative Smoothing and Clinical Wisdom," in *Narrative Psychology: The Storied Nature of Human Conduct*, ed. Theodore R. Sabin (New York: Praeger Special Studies, 1986), 211–232. Print.

19. Polkinghorne, "Narrative Configuration."

20. Quoted in Nancy Zeller, "Narrative Strategies for Case Reports," *International Journal of Qualitative Studies in Education* 8, no. 1 (1995): 85. Print.

2   Lasting Impressions

Memories of a Fulbright Lecturer in China from 1980–1982

Tim Maciel

Introduction

Many sections of Tianjin, the third-largest city in China, were in rubble following the earthquake that occurred four years prior to our arrival in 1980. However, the Foreign Experts Residence at Tianjin University (commonly referred to as "TianDa") was brand new, with spacious bedrooms, private bathrooms, and a clean and bright dining hall and foyer. The residence was built to accommodate the first cohort of Fulbright Lecturers allowed in the country as well as other "foreign experts" who would come throughout my two years in Tianjin. The three of us Americans in Tianjin were among about a dozen or so Fulbrighters placed as foreign experts in institutions across the country.

I write this nearly forty years after first landing in the PRC. I write it solely from memory since my boxes of "China Stuff" in the basement of my home in Vermont contain photo slides, ceramics, an abacus, Chinese language texts, and other memorabilia but no diaries of my experiences as a young 32-year-old college teacher during that remarkable time in China's history. To say that it was a profound experience in my life is an understatement. It left me with a deep understanding of the country and its culture (though in two years, one can only scratch the surface of any culture as foreign to Westerners as China's) and with a great fondness for the many individuals there who impacted my life. Today, when I read about events in China, I cannot help but remember those who were part of my life. I wonder how they are now doing in a country that has prospered and grown in so many ways. Unfortunately, I lost contact with nearly all the Chinese I once knew in Tianjin. Not long after I left in 1982, I took a position in a refugee camp in the Philippines and correspondence even with my family in California was sporadic. Moreover, China had just opened up to the US, and regular mail correspondence with an American would certainly have been noticed in a country that was still emerging from that tragic period known as the Great Proletarian Cultural Revolution.

My Fulbright experience was similar to other overseas experiences in that it required a reevaluation of the norms of my own culture and conduct. I would not say that I became particularly "enlightened" in any way, but the experience certainly deepened and strengthened my sensitivity to other interpretations, justifications of behaviors, and ways of life in China and the world. The mission of the Fulbright Program to promote international peace and understanding requires persistence and an enduring effort in trying to make sense of the world. The value of my experience as a Fulbrighter has extended to this day to the ways I view myself, my culture, and the world.

Pre-Departure Orientation

Our pre-departure orientation in DC focused on the horrors and chaos of the Cultural Revolution and the history and structure of Chinese higher education. China was finally opening up to the world, and the US was now a "friend." While we were thoroughly briefed on Chinese history and politics, far less attention was given to the keys to understanding Chinese culture: Confucianism, Taoism, and the concepts of "guanxi," face, and harmony.

I imagine it was difficult then to present a clear picture of what it was like to be a Chinese professor in China in 1980, so soon after a ten-year period that saw "intellectuals" killed or sent to reeducation camps in the countryside. The Cultural Revolution saw millions of young radicals shutting down schools, destroying religious relics, and banning literature and film and all things tied to the West. A cult of personality grew around Mao Tse Tung, who launched the revolution in 1966 to purge the country of the bourgeois and destroy the "Four Olds"—old ideas, old customs, old culture, and old habits. It is estimated that 1.5 million lives were lost, and 20 million more people were banished. Shortly after our arrival, the Communist Party condemned the Cultural Revolution, placing the blame on the Gang of Four, but to this day, discussion of that period of Chinese history is still frowned on or outright forbidden.

Pre-departure orientation was followed by more briefings at the US Embassy in Beijing. It was also a chance to get to know my fellow Fulbright "TianDa" team members. In the air-conditioned mini-van that brought us down to Tianjin, we worked out final details for structuring and evaluating the program. "Anticipate the difficult by managing the easy," wrote Lao Tzu.

Living Accommodations ("A Roommate? Uh, Let's Talk")

I wish I could say that we made a wonderful first impression upon our arrival, but it did not take long for American individualism and a fierce need for privacy to result in an unpleasant exchange with the university's Foreign

Affairs Office, the *waiban*, the non-academic, political side of the institution that was charged with handling all matters related to Fulbright lecturers and other foreign experts. The first issue was over room accommodations. Our rooms were newly constructed and luxurious by any standard in China with private bathrooms, hot water, and spacious bedrooms complete with desks, reading lamps, and prints of Chinese landscapes. In contrast, students at the university were packed six to eight in single rooms, not much different than one-room brick or cement-block structures that housed large families in this city of over seven million residents. However, when the *waiban* told us that we would need to share our rooms with other foreign experts who would be visiting the university later on in the year, there was immediate protest. A call was quickly made to our US Embassy contact. "What was agreed to regarding room sharing?"

"Well, we didn't get into that level of detail," was the reply. "We're still working out the details. Let's just see what happens."

I can only imagine the consternation of the *waiban*, who were trying to make us as comfortable as possible. "What do they have against sharing a room as spacious and luxurious as these are?" they must have wondered. As it turned out, we never had to double-up our rooms anyway since there were enough single-room accommodations for all the foreign experts who came and went throughout the year. So we survived the first of many cultural stumbles even if we might have contributed to an image of the spoiled American. We acted somewhat obliviously to the culture of China, where Confucian harmony in building relationships is paramount. Moreover, we had yet to learn about "guanxi," which can best be described as the complex network of trust-based relationships that individuals cultivate with other individuals. "Guanxi" is how things get done in China and depends on maintaining harmony and balance. In those first days in China, we were somewhat off balance.

My previous experience as a Peace Corps volunteer in South Korea had somewhat prepared me for life in a Confucian society. I had lived with a family in a small fishing town on the southeast coast and taught ESL. I was the sole Westerner in a town of about 10,000. One invaluable lesson my nearly four years in Korea taught me was, in a Tao sense, to "flow like water," to be flexible and expect the unexpected. The possibility of sharing such a luxurious suite with another person, particularly on a short-term basis, just didn't seem like such a terrible imposition. After all, we had hot water and private bathrooms and a dining room that served us excellent meals (albeit with "healthy" amounts of MSG). This first encounter did remind me that part of the challenge of living in China was not only adjusting to a vastly different culture and language but also adjusting to life in a residence with fellow Americans, most of whom turned out to be amazing individuals whom I liked and respected. However, some took their roles as "foreign experts" far too seriously.

I recall a conversation with our US Embassy liaison at a holiday party in Beijing. "So what's one of the unexpected challenges you've come across in handling this first Fulbright Program in China?" I asked.

She took a drink of her wine, shook her head slowly, and lamented, "I thought we'd have many more issues between the Fulbrighters and their host institutions," she said, "but most of the problems have more to do with Fulbrighters getting along with each other!"

The setting for our program was Tianjin University, established in 1895 and one of the first modern institutions of higher education in China. A large multidisciplinary engineering school with many thousands of students, it was one of first to host international exchanges. Here, we taught groups of thirty college-level teachers who were living far away from their spouses and children for twenty-week programs. They faced countless challenges. Some of our younger professors had to leave their children back in their home provinces many hours away, but even outside the program, it was not unusual for married couples to be separated with one spouse working in one city and the other in a city many miles away. It was never clear to us whether our students had any choice in attending the program or how they were selected. When we asked the *waiban*, the response was something like, "They are very happy to be here." We soon came to appreciate the adage: "Ask a Western question, get an Eastern answer."

Our students shared drab rooms with cold cement floors with their roommates on the TianDa campus. In class, whenever I said something like, "Oh, Mr. Shin, you must miss your wife and new baby back in Hunan province," the response was predictable: "I am very happy to learn English from you. I want to do my best to help our country." Mr. Shin and his classmates were just getting to know each other too, but undoubtedly, their culture of Confucianism and Taoism—and the real threat of public criticism—made them much more strategic in their public behavior in and outside class. Over time, I came to understand that Chinese relationships were determined and greatly influenced by age, status, prestige, and standing. All these factors were calibrated when determining how to behave, even when answering questions I had thought were so innocuous. I had so much to learn.

The Job (From "Nyet" to "Yes")

Our job descriptions were straightforward. We would teach English as a Foreign Language (EFL) and EFL teaching methods to groups of college-level English teachers who would come from institutions all over northeast China for twenty-week intensive programs. On average, about thirty teachers would be included in each program, and so our class size was ideal, about ten to a class. Classes were five days a week for five hours a day. That was about all we had to go on when we first arrived. I had presumed that our students would have a wide range of competency in the language but was surprised by how wide that range turned out to be. Some were former Russian language instructors who had nearly zero competency in English but had been told that they would now be teaching English (Russian, English, what's the difference?). We placed these students in beginning level ESL classes. Others were nearly fluent and had previous experience teaching English as a Foreign Language before the Cultural Revolution or had worked in some capacity with English-speaking foreigners. For these students, we designed classes in applied linguistics and ESL teaching methods and strategies. Then there were others who fell somewhere between these extremes and to whom we taught intermediate or advanced ESL combined with some teaching methodology.

In addition to providing language lessons, we distributed and introduced our students to dozens of ESL textbooks and ESL readers. Each student was also given a small library of literary works—simplified for second-language learners—by American writers such as Edgar Allan Poe, O. Henry, and Emily Dickinson. It was like Christmas for our students each time we distributed boxes of texts delivered from the embassy.

In my first program, I naively believed that we would have a positive impact on the quality of instruction in Chinese college and university ESL programs. I believed our focus on communicative approaches to language learning, on student-centered practices and motivational techniques along with empirical methods of measuring language proficiency might actually make a dent in the grammar translation method that was the stock in trade of EFL classes in China in 1980. My optimism began to wane, however, when I began asking my students to provide feedback on the program. At times, they would exasperate me with their indirect form of communication, but at other times, they would be brutally candid. Conversations on the program went something like this:

ME: So, Mr. Li, we're almost finished with the program. I hope it's helped you.

MR. LI: Oh, you and the others have been so kind. And you work so hard to teach us.

ME: Do you think you'll use any of the materials we gave you or use any of the teaching strategies and techniques we introduced to you?

MR. LI: Oh, no! We must teach the same as all the other teachers in my institution.

ME: Hmm. So why do you think your country and mine have these teacher training programs?

MR. LI: I think so we can understand English better. Your ways are interesting, but our students are used to the way Chinese teach English.

ME: Ah! *"Xiànzài zhīdàole"* ("I understand now").

Eventually, in my career, I came to realize that methodology was a small part of the equation for student success in language courses. I came to understand that an effective learning experience depends primarily on the relationships between the student and the subject matter; the professor and the subject matter; and the student and the professor. In other words, if the student comes to the class highly motivated to learn, chances are good that he or she will learn. If the professor is passionate about her or his subject matter, but has little or no connection with the students, the chances are still good that that professor's passion will inspire the students to learn. And if the students and the professor form a good relationship and if that professor takes an interest in each student's learning, then the chances are excellent that the students will, indeed, learn. And if all three relationships happen, the outcome could very well be a magical learning experience.

In China in 1980, less than 1% of the population engaged in higher learning. These were, then, highly motivated, intelligent students. They would learn. Despite the Cultural Revolution that denigrated "intellectualism" so brutally, a Confucian tradition that so highly values teaching and learning persisted. It is tradition that dictates that a teacher achieve perfection in her or his craft, a tradition in which the Chinese teacher takes pride in the profession and strives to master her or his field. For Confucius, a teacher had to be willing to do her or his best just as a student must want to learn; otherwise, the teacher cannot use "rotten wood (as it) cannot be carved" as the common Chinese phrase goes. And so even if our students could not employ innovative methods in the classroom, I believe that most of them strove to master the field, even within the strict confines of a conformist and tightly controlled system.

Saturday Lectures (and Self-Indulgences)

In addition to weekday ESL lessons, the three of us took turns on Saturdays presenting ninety-minute lectures on the culture of the United States. These were presented to large audiences that included students and professors at TianDa as well as from other institutions. I wish I could say that our Fulbright team coordinated a cohesive series of lectures with common themes on American history, culture, and politics; but instead, we followed our Western inclinations and individually decided on topics that struck our fancy. These were "extras" that the *waiban* had coerced us into doing for TianDa and that made the weekends a little more interesting for our students.

At times, the lecture hall was filled with over three hundred Chinese anxious to gain our perspectives on the United States, "Meiguo" (literally "Beautiful Country"). I enjoyed lecturing with an interpreter since the pauses during translations allowed time for me to consider my next statement.

Lectures generally included topics such as "Twentieth Century US History," "Checks and Balances and the Structure of American Government," the ever popular "Food and Holidays in America," and more indulgent topics, such as "Mark Twain and American Identity" (Huck following his heart of hearts in helping a slave escape to freedom—the spirit of anarchy!). We had a tacit agreement with the *waiban* to avoid current events and controversial topics, such as the Iranian hostage crisis. Nevertheless, during my second year at TianDa, I felt the need to really self-indulge and throw caution and discretion to the wind. I delivered a lecture entitled "The Sexual, Political, and Social Revolution of the '60's." I have no idea what the nearly three hundred Chinese attending the lecture must have thought when I played lines from anti-war tunes and spoke about the Vietnam protest movement and Woodstock. The only feedback I got was from Mrs. Shin of the *waiban*. "That was very interesting," she said with a wry smile. Enough said. My next lecture was a less provocative discussion of "The Geography of the United States."

The Foreign Experts' Residence

In 1980, we had no laptops or personal computers, no cell phones, and no social media. What we did have to occupy our free time were endless conversations with each other and other foreign guests. Discussions inevitably led to comparisons and contrasts between "our" social, economic, and political systems and "theirs," between Eastern and Western thought, values, and ideologies. Then there were endless conversations about the language and culture. I had the joy of studying Chinese three times a week at the residence with a tutor, Mrs. Chun, a sweet, elderly professor who seemed genuinely thrilled whenever I displayed the most rudimentary progress in spoken Chinese. I have never met a kinder, more patient instructor anywhere.

The residence had a constant flow of experts from a variety of fields who would come for short periods to share their expertise, particularly in technical fields, such as engineering and agriculture. It was not uncommon to share meals with remarkable experts in their field, such as Herbert Simon, a Nobel Prize–winning economist whom I recall was unguardedly sanguine about the future of China even in those uncertain times. We had such a variety of visitors, socialists and capitalists, scientists and authors, each trying to make sense of a country emerging from over a decade of international seclusion. It was a fun place to be.

On occasion, our students came to visit us at the residence, always in groups and always with a leader who would come with a sheet of written questions about life in America. Sometimes, these questions revealed how broad the cultural gap truly was: "Why do Americans love their pets more than their children?" and "Why are factory owners allowed to make so much more money than their workers?" I recall one student, without a hint of malice, asked me if I would buy medicine for my mother if she were gravely sick. These were students who had been exposed to a decade of daily vilifications of the West, and so I should not have been surprised when they asked why Americans let our old people die alone and impoverished in old age homes.

I tried to be candid about what I saw as failings in our society and spoke about the discrimination that many Americans faced, particularly minorities, women, and the poor. I spoke about upward movement in the US and how children of immigrants, like my own father and many like him, were still able to achieve economic success while also doing good for their communities. But I also shared my perception that the "American Dream" was still unattainable for many. I spoke about the freedoms Americans enjoyed but also how many families were stuck in cycles of poverty and suffered from injustices in an imperfect system. Since there was virtually no back and forth, I have no idea how my views were interpreted. I tried to convey the fact that these were "my" own opinions alone and that I was not a "cultural ambassador" who could speak for a diverse population of over 250 million, a quarter the size of China's own immense population. I explained how I often found fault with government policies but remember one student being thoroughly confused as to how I could work for a government program and not fully support that government. Through it all, my hope was that with continued interpersonal contact, some of the gross misunderstandings and biases against American "foreign devils" would eventually be tempered by more realistic and favorable viewpoints.

Excursions, Spring Break, and the Joyous Return of My Sock

Our *waiban* was extraordinarily generous in arranging excursions to cultural events and industries around Tianjin. We were taken to performances of the Peking Opera, factories, and, during vacation breaks, on tours around the country. One of our first excursions was to the Tianjin Flying Pigeon kite factory. A van loaded up about a half dozen foreign guests, and off we went to observe workers assembling and packaging beautiful kites of all shapes and sizes. After the tour, we gathered for tea and cookies and were asked if we had any questions. Oh, we had many: "How are workers chosen for these jobs?" "What is their work and vacation schedule like?"

"Are profits reinvested back into the factory?" "How does one become a manager?" But it did not turn out to be the kind of free-flowing exchange we had anticipated. Our host jotted down the first question and then asked if we had others. More questions were posed, and each time, with no response, the question was written into a notebook. We were then told to enjoy the refreshments while the factory leaders left to discuss our questions to ensure, we were told, that we would hear the correct response. With kites in hand, we left a little better informed and were once again reminded how conformity of thought was the rule of the day.

During our first spring break, the *waiban* sent us on a wonderful two-week tour around the country with a personal "guide," Mr. Kim. We were treated like honored dignitaries as we traveled by train from Tianjin to Beijing and then on to Xi'an, Chengdu, Guilin, Kunming, Wuhan, Suzhou, Shanghai, and Nanjing. It was an unforgettable experience. In Xi'an, we were among the first to see the army of terracotta warriors that had just been excavated. We floated down the Yangtze through the famous Three Gorges, witnessing spectacular scenery and watching fishermen with trained cormorants catching fish just as they had been doing for thousands of years. We were taken to the fabulous Lingyin monastery in Hangzhou with its breathtaking temples, giant Buddhist statues, rock carvings, and pagodas. In Shanghai, as in so many other cities, we were stunned by the density of the population as we shuffled along the Bund, marveling at the colonial architecture of the 1800s, a time when the streets were teeming with human-powered rickshaws carrying foreigners and wealthy Chinese through the masses of humanity.

It was an amazing trip, one that made me feel privileged to be among the first group of Fulbrighters in this fascinating country. Weeks later, back in Tianjin, I was reminded of how safe the country was when the *waiban* delivered a package to me with a belt, a ball pen, and a single sock, items that I had forgotten in hotels during the trip. In 1980, China was one of the safest places in the world for foreign guests. Pickpocketing, assaults, robberies, and other crimes must surely have existed, but foreign guests—men and women alike—felt completely safe. Perhaps having "keepers" tracking our every move had something to do with it, but even traveling alone around the country, which I did extensively after my second year, I felt completely safe, as did other foreign guests I encountered on my travels.

Secret Encounters ("I Need to Tell You This")

It was no secret that our students were not allowed to speak with us privately in one-to-one conversations. We learned, too, that if a student said something in class or at a social function that was "incorrect," the others were obligated to report that student to the *waiban*. This fact of life made conversation classes a challenge even when we tried to focus on safe, innocuous topics. For our students, who had survived the vicissitudes of life as academics and who now found themselves being taught by those who were so recently considered "foreign devils," it was understandable that they would approach the experience with extreme caution. Yet, inevitably, in every program, there were those intrepid souls who surreptitiously sought me out to tell me stories of how they were persecuted during the Cultural Revolution, how professors were tossed out of third-floor windows by the Red Guard, and how they nearly starved when masses of "intellectuals" were forced out of the cities into the countryside. My first such encounter came when I was crossing the campus one cold evening and was met by one of my students. "I need to tell you this," he began and continued to describe the tragic death of his father at the hands of the Red Guard.

Not long after my Fulbright experience in China, I worked in the Philippines at a refugee processing center serving thousands of Vietnamese, Lao, and Khmer refugees who had fled their homelands after the war. There, too, individuals would sometimes tell their own stories of horror and violence. Like for my Chinese students in Tianjin, it seemed to be part of the grieving process, a catharsis that allowed them to move forward in their lives.

Breaking the Ice (and Not Falling In)

One of the most basic of cultural differences an American experiences in China is the contrast between individualism and collectivism. A feature of capitalist societies is the notion of individualism, the principle that individual effort is rewarded and the individual reaps the benefits of this effort. In stark contrast, a feature of socialist ideology is the notion of the good of the collective over the individual. This was a theme that was repeated over and over again. Never did I hear a student lament about the hardships of being separated from family or children or aging parents to be in the program. Who can say if they got tired of cooking noodles over small hotplates every night? Instead, they constantly expressed gratitude and delight for the opportunity to study with us to serve their country. Harmony! The notion of sacrificing one's own needs for the motherland is hardly alien to those of us in Western cultures, but most of us will not deny the high premium many Americans place on the individual pursuit of happiness over the collective good.

A trait of any culture is the notion that "our" values and views of the world are both the norm and the ideal, and others are really, at heart, just like us or, if not, they wish they could be like us. Intercultural understanding reveals the utter fallacy of these notions. Cultures are different, and societies have very different values and worldviews even if we do share many universal and human values, like love and respect for our parents and children. In China, I found myself continually searching for those similarities and differences. I hoped, in some way, to build trusting relationships with my students, the *waiban*, and other Chinese I encountered, even knowing that it takes time to break down preconceived ideas and knowing that we were just getting to know one another.

In hindsight, I see that I might have underestimated the fact that we were merely breaking the ice for further exchanges. The Fulbright mission was then—and still is—to increase mutual understanding between the people of the United States and those of other countries. Given the great chasm of mutual *mis*understanding that existed between China and the United States in 1980, on a small and very personal level, I believe we made progress, but, more importantly, we laid the groundwork for a Fulbright Program that, as later chapters in this book shall show, is still thriving. I take satisfaction, then, in being part of a group that didn't "blow it" in the beginning (despite those occasional Saturday morning rants!). I like to believe that when I left China in 1982, some "guanxi" was built not just between the Chinese I came to know and me but also between our two countries.

Rapid Change

During my second year in Tianjin, a remarkable change occurred literally overnight: suddenly, the streets, parks, and other open areas were flooded with farmers selling fish, vegetables, and produce. Orderly lines of men and women waited patiently to purchase cabbage, carrots, and other food items. These items were sold in small shops before, but it was the sudden proliferation and abundance of fresh food that stunned us. I later found out that this was the result of a series of economic reforms termed "Socialism with Chinese Characteristics" that Deng Xiaoping had initiated two years earlier. The reforms introduced market principles to the country and involved the decollectivization of agriculture and permission for farmers to engage in private business. It was one of many economic reforms to come.

When I returned to the United States for a visit after my first year in China, I remember how taken aback I was by the intense, ubiquitous nature of our consumer society. I was struck by the constant, inescapable barrage of advertising in all its forms and for an endless variety of goods and services. Cars, fast food, pharmaceuticals, phone services, sporting goods—thousands of items flood our consciousness 24/7. Until one escapes it, it is hard to appreciate how much it is part of American life.

I remember the mixed feelings I had seeing a Kentucky Fried Chicken restaurant with a Colonel Sanders figure standing in front of a shop in

Chengdu when I returned to China in 1991, nine years after completing my second year as a Fulbrighter. I had returned to work on a Peace Corps program in Szechuan province. I was stunned by how much the country had changed. The streets were still jammed with huge crowds of people, but now women had colorful shirts and different hairstyles. There were Western-style department stores with perfume and clothing from Europe and the US. To be sure, the level of consumerism did not even approach that in the West, but what a radical change from the day piles of eggplants and tomatoes suddenly appeared for sale in Tianjin! Socialism with Chinese characteristics!

Today, whether it is through professional work, involvement in local politics, penning letters to our local newspaper, or merely making calls to my Congressional delegation on various issues, I believe I am continuing and extending my Fulbright experience and am, in some way, still promoting international peace and understanding by giving voice to uniquely acquired knowledge. I trust, too, that Fulbright Programs in China today are benefiting from the "guanxi" we established during those initial two years in that remarkable land.

3 Transformations in Understanding

Lessons on Self and Culture from Teaching Abroad

Jesse Butler

For the 2016–2017 academic year, I taught sophomore-level philosophy courses on self-knowledge and American culture at Jinan University in Guangzhou, China. I was there, along with my wife and our two children, as a visiting US Fulbright scholar. This was our first time to China, as well as Asia more generally, and we dove in head first to live amid a culture and environment that was dramatically different from what we knew in our life at home in Arkansas. In this narrative inquiry, I will investigate to what extent this year abroad could be considered a "transformative experience," in the sense discussed by philosopher L. A. Paul: "Having a transformative experience teaches you something new, something that you could not have known before having the experience, while also changing you as a person."[1] There are many ways in which our year in China could be considered to be a transformative experience. We learned things we did not anticipate. We shared amazing experiences that shaped who we are as a family, and each of our lives was impacted in ways we will never forget. For this particular inquiry into the Fulbright experience, however, I will focus on my primary role as a teacher and offer a narrative inquiry as to whether I might be a different teacher now, with a new understanding of my students and what I teach them, as a result of my experiences with Chinese students in the classroom.

The courses I taught in China were based upon a new interdisciplinary and cross-cultural course on self-knowledge I developed through an "Enduring Questions" grant from the National Endowment for the Humanities.[2] I taught two versions of the course at my home institution and decided that it would be a worthwhile course to teach abroad as well. I chose to apply for a Fulbright teaching program geared toward courses on the United States for students in China, which led me to develop a version of the course emphasizing sections on American conceptions of self and identity. I taught four sections of the course during my year in China, two sections each semester, resulting in the experiences that follow. I taught the course in English, as an elective option for students taking courses in English through the International School at Jinan University. I will not detail all aspects of the class, nor will I distinguish between the different sections of the course I taught. Instead, for the purposes of this narrative, I will synthesize my experiences together in terms of their overall impact on my teaching and my understanding of my students, in parallel with the general course content and structure.

On my first day of class, I followed the customary practice of introducing the course by giving the students a syllabus and explaining the basic procedures and requirements. This is not a particularly exciting way to start a course, but I thought it would be important to begin by giving the students an idea of how things would work. I had been told by past Fulbrighters that education in China typically follows an authoritarian lecture format, with the students exposed to passive lectures followed by systematic exams to test their memorization of the course content. Since I teach classes in a rather different manner, I thought I should begin by telling the students how the course would be conducted.

The students all arrived on time and were sitting attentively at their desks when my first class began. They were quiet, but I detected a sense of excited anticipation from their expressions. I began class by introducing myself, explaining how I had come to China through the Fulbright Program, and then proceeded to explain what the course would be about and how it would work. The students remained quiet and attentive throughout, just as I had expected from what I had been told beforehand about teaching in China. However, they surprised me at the end of the class. When I wrapped up my introduction and told them we were finished for the day, they did not ask any questions. Nor did they simply pack up and leave. Instead, they applauded together, with enthusiastic smiles shining back at me.

In America, after going over a syllabus on the first day of class, the typical response is to get some questions about how difficult the course will be and how grades will be determined: "Will we get essay exam questions in advance?" "Will there be any extra credit?" But my Chinese students asked no such questions. Instead, they seemed to simply accept what I told them they would be doing in the course and then happily applauded the class in return. To be clear, it wasn't just the applause per se that was especially surprising. The surprising thing was that it was in response to the course requirements. These students applauded the fact that I would be asking them to read difficult material for nearly every class and to complete substantial writing assignments with the expectation of understanding and applying the material, all in a foreign language. I knew in that moment that this would be a very different kind of teaching experience.

The first writing assignment I gave was a short exploratory essay. I asked my students to imagine that they had been adopted at birth by an American family and raised in the US rather than China and then to reflect upon whether or not they would be the same person as they are now in their current life. This was a new assignment, specifically designed for my course in China, but I had explored similar topics with my students in America. Many of my American students, convinced that their identity is constituted by an immutable eternal soul, would say that no such cultural shift would substantially change who they are at the most fundamental level. Sameness of soul entails being the same person, regardless of how variable one's culture and upbringing may be. Some students draw a similar conclusion but on the basis of their genetic makeup, identifying themselves with their biological nature. Others, however, are inclined to give a more foundational role to cultural conditioning, allowing for the possibility that the nurture side of things can fundamentally shape one's identity. Before reading on, it might be interesting for you yourself to reflect on this question. Are you a product of your cultural conditioning, such that you would have been a different person if you had been raised in a different cultural environment? Or is there some more fundamental aspect of your identity that would constitute you being the same person, regardless of cultural variation? What would you say? What would you guess my Chinese students said?

Overwhelmingly, most of my Chinese students said they would have been different people if they had been raised in America. This in itself was not surprising. Eastern cultures are known for their collectivism, with priority given to the group, in contrast to the individualism associated with the West, where the individual self is given priority over the group. For example, the influential social psychologist Richard Nisbett describes this difference as so pronounced that Easterners and Westerners live in different worlds: "East Asians live in an interdependent world in which the self is part of a larger whole; Westerners live in a world in which the self is a unitary free agent."[3] Having been steeped in academic literature by Nisbett and others emphasizing the collectivism of Eastern cultures, I expected that my students would be inclined to give priority to the power of culture in shaping their identities as people, and indeed this was confirmed by their essay responses. The vast majority of my students said they would be different people if they had been raised in America.

There were a few exceptions who said that a change in culture would not result in a change in identity, however. These exceptional responses shared a single revealing factor in their answer: They all adopted the idea of an immaterial soul, just as the majority of my American students do, yet in this case, these students were in the minority. None of my Chinese students considered that they could be the same person by virtue of having the same genetic makeup, regardless of cultural upbringing, even though that is another option available on the map of possibilities. Of course, these observations are only anecdotal, but I found the absence of a genetic conception of identity interesting, especially given that this was at a university with active programs in medicine and the biological sciences. Be that as it may, I was not surprised to find that almost all of my students said they would be different people had they been adopted and raised in America, given the collectivist emphasis on group identity typically associated with Chinese culture, including both its longstanding Confucian heritage throughout history and the current Communism of the People's Republic of China.

What I was surprised about, however, were the details of the changes they described. Many of my students fantasized that they would have had more freedom as Americans, envisioning that they would have been able to choose who they were. Some said that they could have become stars on YouTube, exhibiting their individuality on social media as popular gamers or musicians. Some envisioned themselves as famous athletes, while others simply imagined that they would have had more free time to spend with their friends and do what they wanted, less encumbered by educational demands and parental expectations. These responses surprised me in terms of how much of American culture they had imbibed, largely through popular movies, television programs, and so forth. Like many of my American students, they too had bought into the American Dream of individual freedom and controlling one's own destiny through one's own intentions and choices, only they lacked the reality check of failed promise that some of my former students were showing me with their more cynical Facebook posts back home, as they confronted difficult job markets and contentious contemporary politics.

Despite initial apparent differences, as well as their own views of how different they are from Americans, the overall behavior of my students in China gradually began to appear remarkably similar to that of my students in America. They dressed in contemporary American fashion, with English labels and slogans prominently appearing on their clothes. They also all had cell phones, and they were obsessively entranced by life on the screen, constantly communicating with each other through the all-pervasive social media platform in China: WeChat. As the initial allure of having a foreign instructor from America subsided, I found myself asking students to put their phones away during class. A few of them explained that they were using their phones to help with translation, which I decided to allow, but the overall techno-enchantment appeared quite the same as what I was accustomed to at home. This too was a surprise. I expected my students in China to be noticeably different in their classroom behaviors, suspecting that a more authoritarian education model might have relieved me from needing to tell them to put away their phones during class time, but that is not what I found. They were young people caught up in the allure of new technology and social media, just like my students in America.

They were less accustomed to in-class discussion, however, and this was a difference for which I had planned. I give a fair amount of lecture content in my courses, in order to convey central concepts and theories and so forth, but I more prominently emphasize active engagement through in-class discussion, asking my students questions and getting them to share and compare their various answers with one another in open free-form discussion. I already knew that this was not common in the Chinese educational system, so I expected that I would need to acclimate my students in China to my open-discussion style of teaching. They were quiet at first, just as I had expected, but once I made it clear that discussion was an important part of the class, I was surprised by how enthusiastically they took to a discussion-based class format.

In America, I am accustomed to having a number students who readily engage in class discussion, while a relatively equal number sit quietly in either passive observation or jaded antipathy to class activities. I did not detect the jaded types in any of my classes in China, however. They all seemed happy to be in school, genuinely appreciative of the opportunities afforded to them through being at a major university. Moreover, they were ripe for talking, openly sharing their thoughts and experiences in ways that I did not expect. Not everyone was talkative, but overall, they took to open class discussion quite readily and naturally. In fact, many students were not shy about bringing up personal details about their lives, nor were they afraid to disagree with each other or even me as their instructor, especially after I made it clear that an important part of philosophy is discussing differences of opinion and challenging the ideas of others. After gaining my permission to do so, they bluntly told me when they disagreed with me— my interpretations of Confucian philosophy did not always match theirs, for instance, and they openly shared their thoughts with me and each other, revealing a capacity for individual expression and open exchange of ideas that matched what I had become accustomed to with my more engaged students in America.

One of the first reading assignments I gave to my students was a chapter about cultural influences on cognition, from a book on the power of culture written by contemporary American philosopher Jesse Prinz. Following the common academic emphasis on differences between Eastern and Western cultures, my students read how "Some countries, like the United States, are extremely individualistic, and some, like China, are extremely collectivist."[4] Not having discussed this idea with many people from China before, I was very curious to see how my students would respond. When I asked them in class whether they thought this statement about China and the US was true, they strongly and emphatically agreed. In fact, they too had been taught the same idea already, although from rather different sources.

Their own cultural education and upbringing, through classes on Communism and Confucianism, utilized the same distinction between individualism and collectivism and taught them the value and importance of being a citizen in a collectivist society. Also, as mentioned previously, they were aware of America's own identification with individualism and the celebration of individual freedom in popular media from America, which likewise confirmed the dichotomy in their understanding, just as it does with many Americans in their own self-understanding.

So, most of my Chinese students thought they would be different people if they had been raised in a different culture, confirming belief in the centrality of culture in shaping identity, and they also told me they identified as collectivists while also viewing Americans as individualists. Does this confirm the collectivism versus individualism dichotomy as a foundational difference between the East and the West? It certainly seems to do so on the surface, if we take these observations at face value. As any good critical thinker knows, however, we cannot simply seek to identify confirmation of a claim in establishing its truth. That would make us prone to confirmation bias, selectively cherry-picking information that confirms what we are investigating while relevant disconfirming information may go unnoticed. Was there any information in my experiences with my Chinese students that might disconfirm the common conception that Western culture is individualistic while Eastern culture is collectivist in nature? Indeed, there was. Even though my students thought of themselves as collectivists, they not only behaved as unique individuals with their own thoughts and interests; they did so in ways that were remarkably parallel to the behaviors of my American students at home. They were also drawn to American culture and its supposed individualism, which they integrated into their own understanding of themselves in very interesting ways as the course progressed.

One central module of my self-knowledge course is on the topic of the "self-made" person in American culture, looking at the writings and lives of exemplary "self-made" people in American history, such as Benjamin Franklin, Frederick Douglass, and Sojourner Truth. This content is dry and boring to many of my American students, who have already been exposed to the ideas throughout their education, but it was one of the most successful and popular sections of the course in China. In fact, the majority of my students wrote their final papers on the topic, even though they had a variety of other options to choose from, demonstrating a strong attraction to the idea of freely defining one's own identity.

In introducing this topic to my students, I had them read a portion of Benjamin Franklin's autobiography, where he describes his own efforts toward shaping himself into a virtuous person. In this famous passage, Franklin documents his behavior in relation to key virtues he wishes to establish in himself, only to find that he was incapable of achieving the level of perfection that he originally sought.[5] On the surface, Franklin's project for achieving moral perfection appears to fit the stereotype of American individualism, with an individual seeking to define himself through his own thoughts and actions. Franklin self-selected a set of virtues he wanted to cultivate and systematically monitored his own behavior toward that end. This is how I introduced and explained Franklin's project, and it is also what attracted many of my students to use Franklin's project as an example for their own self-reflections in their final papers.

However, some interesting counterpoints to Franklin's apparent individualism emerged in our class exploration of the topic. For example, several students brought out the fact that Franklin had relied on other people in central aspects of his project. One of his chosen virtues, humility, is defined by the command to "Imitate Jesus and Socrates," which my students interpreted as a kind of deference to elders as authorities. Franklin does not explain why he defined humility in this manner, and Western readers who are familiar with Jesus and Socrates as iconic individuals in their own right might simply see the choice as further supporting an individualistic paradigm, but to my Chinese students, the description seemed more strongly cultural and hierarchical, illustrating a kind of social reverence to prominent exemplars in the history of one's own culture.

Moreover, Franklin states that he added that particular virtue to his list through an insight he gained from the observations of another person:

> [A] Quaker Friend having kindly inform'd me that I was generally thought proud; that my Pride show'd itself frequently in Conversation; that I was not content with being in the right when discussing any Point, but was overbearing & rather insolent; of which he convinc'd me by mentioning several Instances;—I determined endeavouring to cure myself if I could of this Vice or Folly among the rest, and I added Humility to my List, giving an extensive Meaning to the Word.[6]

While Franklin describes this as a choice he himself made and implemented in his own self-chosen project, it stood out to my Chinese students as a lesson that was fundamentally dependent upon the social context of learning from another person. Franklin had learned something about himself not by his own efforts but rather through a social relationship.

Adding further to a more socially oriented reading of Franklin's project, several of my students discovered research suggesting that Franklin himself may have been influenced by Confucian philosophy. Of course, I was aware of the general commonality shared by both Franklin and Confucius regarding the cultivation of virtue, but I was unaware that Confucianism itself as a distinct worldview may have played a role in Franklin's own understanding of virtue. He does not mention Confucius or China anywhere in his autobiography, but according to the research of Dave Wang, Franklin and other American founders drew upon Confucian moral philosophy in the development of their thoughts on virtuous citizenship.[7] To be clear, I am not an intellectual historian and have not evaluated the strength of Wang's case. I find it intriguing, but his evidence is somewhat piecemeal, indicating some interest in Confucianism but perhaps not necessarily a foundational influence. Regardless, however, what I want to point out here is the fact that my Chinese students sought out this research on their own, exhibiting a curiosity toward relating this material about an American icon to their own culture. Despite the fact that they readily identified America with individualism and China with collectivism, they identified and latched onto an underlying commonality that brought them together in their understanding of human life.[8]

Many of the students found Franklin's project in self-cultivation interesting and valuable, but even more were inspired by Emerson's classic "Self-Reliance." When I've had American students read Emerson's essay, they often complain of its length and wordiness. However, despite the fact that it was the longest single reading assignment of the semester, with verbose language and sometimes confusing terminology, my Chinese students were captivated by its message of shirking convention and following one's own heart. They saw in Emerson the same free pursuit of individuality that they earlier imagined themselves having had they been born in America, unfettered by the norms of virtue they saw echoed from their own culture while reading Franklin. They seemed liberated and empowered by Emerson's dictum to "trust thyself," and even though I explained to them that the "self" Emerson had in mind was the same cosmic universal self that we had earlier explored in the *Katha Upanishad* from India,[9] they strongly connected it to their own individual selves and inclinations without the further metaphysical context of unifying oneself with the universe. For them, Emerson was a license to embrace their own individuality, which led to "Self-Reliance" being the most popular course reading they chose to write about in their final essays.

Most of them did not see this as an overt rejection of their own culture, however. Many students connected the individualistic inspiration they drew from Emerson with an equally strong desire to contribute to their society through their anticipated careers and life plans. One student argued that Emerson shared common ground with Neo-Confucian philosophy, for instance, while many others simply conceived of following their own natural aspirations in terms of contributing to the well-being of their fellow citizens as well. Writing in response to a "self-development" essay prompt that asked them to apply the course content to their own lives, multiple students independently drew the same conclusion that it was by following their own hearts and ambitions that they could best serve as contributing members of society. Whether their career goals were nursing or journalism, many of my students portrayed their embrace of self-reliance in relation to the actualization of their individual goals as productive citizens. For the most part, they did not wildly envision themselves or their personal desires in opposition to their collectivist culture but rather as individuals intrinsically motivated to participate in their culture through their own ambitions.

I found this result deeply interesting. I had built this course following the commonly assumed contrast between Western individualism and Eastern collectivism, with numerous readings and observations seeming to confirm this contrast as a fundamental difference in self-understanding between cultures. Yet, beneath the surface were identifiable experiences that challenged it, culminating with a significant number of my self-identifying collectivist Chinese students being drawn toward individualism instead but nevertheless connecting this individualism back to their embedded cultural existence and collective citizenship. Rather than being a fundamental truth about cultural difference, the individualist/collectivist divide was revealed by this experience to be an oversimplification, a false dichotomy projected onto to people who, despite their real and varied cultural differences, were both simultaneously individuals and members of a collective.

To be honest, I already had doubts about the oversimplified nature of the individualism/collectivism dichotomy prior to my year in China, but I continued to frame my course and my understanding by its structure, thinking that, while perhaps too simple, it still tapped into something fundamentally and importantly different between cultures. But as my experiences with my Chinese students unfolded, I became less confident in it and saw its problems vividly rise to the surface of my real-world experience. Through this direct engagement with Chinese students, my experiences while teaching abroad shifted my understanding in a way that I had only dimly glimpsed in an intellectual manner beforehand. I wouldn't say I became a different person myself through this experience, so perhaps it was not a transformative experience in the most profound sense, but it was a transformative experience that shaped both my understanding and my approach to teaching in ways that I did not anticipate. After getting to know my Chinese students and watching them explore their own understanding of themselves, I found it patently absurd to think of them as any less individualistic than my American students. They all, of course, had unique personalities that set them apart from each other as individuals, while also at the same time uniting them as people aiming to making a place for themselves as members of human social life in the contemporary world. Their individualism was deeply connected to their collectivism, highlighting their individuality as components of a larger social tapestry, rather than producing a contrasting antagonism between competing values or conceptions of human existence.

This dissolved unity of the individual within the collective became more evident to me when I returned to teaching in America and saw it applied equally to my American students as well. Rather than seeing them as individualists who could perhaps learn a thing or two by studying collectivist viewpoints from other cultures, as I once had, I saw them as unwitting collectivists despite their avowed conceptions of themselves as unique individuals. Their differences with my Chinese students receded to the background, with their shared traits as contemporary humans coming more prominently to the fore. They are indeed unique individuals but individuals who are deeply subsumed within collectivist cultural structures that have shaped and defined their individuality. They are individuals who define their individuality by participation in group memberships, across religious, political, geographical, gender-based, racial, and pop-cultural categories that form the ingredients of their avowed individuality. Of course, I was aware of these categories and their impact on identity beforehand, but they now stood out to me as a broad and significant collectivist backdrop within which individual identities are shaped, such that America itself could arguably be conceived as being just as collectivist in nature as China.

While there are individualistic aspects of American culture and collectivist aspects of Chinese culture, especially in the explicit avowals of their respective leaders, icons, and citizens, I've come to think that we are far more similar than different, with both individualist and collectivist elements in both cultures existing in one world together. We are not separated by world-lines drawn between individualism and collectivism but rather exist together as beings in a diverse cosmopolitan stew, all floating together on the same planetary ball in space, as similar in our humanity as we are different across our cultural variations. Of course, this evidence is unsystematic and anecdotal, based upon my own idiosyncratic personal experience in a singular globe-trotting event. There could be some selection bias in the types of students who took my course, given that it required a background in English, although English is now widely taught throughout educational systems in China. Relatedly, my experience could be a relatively recent result of increasingly blurred cultural lines produced through the post-colonial processes of international globalization, rather than a more general reflection of human nature across cultures and throughout history. Regardless of its temporal scope, however, it was a concrete observation made quite vivid to me through my time as a visiting teacher abroad in China, teaching unique individuals who connected their individuality to the cultural dynamics through which they lived their lives, which now included me and the ideas I brought to them. I left China feeling less like a foreigner visiting another world and more like a global citizen in a single world shared by all of humanity. That is enough for me to conclude that, despite our differences, we are all individuals simultaneously situated within a broader collective that is not confined by national borders but rather extends throughout our concrete connections across the planet.

Notes

1. L.A. Paul, *Transformative Experience* (New York: Oxford University Press, 2014), 17.
2. Further information about the course is available on the course website: Jesse Butler, "Who Am I? The Perennial Quest for Self-Knowledge," https://sites.google.com/a/uca.edu/self-knowledge/.
3. Richard Nisbett, *The Geography of Thought, How Asians and Westerners Think Differently . . . and Why* (New York: Free Press, 2003), 76.
4. Jesse Prinz, *Beyond Human Nature: How Culture and Experience Shape the Human Mind* (New York: W. W. Norton and Company, 2012), 196.
5. For example, one of his virtues is humility, but he cynically concludes that even if he achieved the virtue of humility, his pride would reemerge in response. Benjamin Franklin, "Project for Moral Perfection from *The Autobiography*," www.whatsoproudlywehail.org.
6. Franklin, 7.
7. Dave Wang, "Confucius in the American Founding: The Founders' Efforts to Use Confucian Moral Philosophy in Their Endeavor to Create New Virtue for the New Nation," *Virginia Review of Asian Studies* 16 (2014): 11–26.
8. It is worth adding here that Confucian philosophy itself may be more individualistic than it is often conceived to be. Leading contemporary Confucian philosopher Tu Weiming, for example, makes a point of emphasizing selfhood and the centrality of individual self-cultivation in his work. From a more nuanced and developed perspective, Confucianism may not stand fundamentally apart from the emphasis on individual development as typically attributed to the West. See Tu Weiming, *Humanity and Self-Cultivation: Essays in Confucian Thought* (Boston: Cheng & Tsui Company, 1998).
9. Juan Mascaró, trans., *The Upanishads* (New York: Penguin Books, 1965).

4   Teaching Library and Information Science as a Fulbright Scholar

Reflections from a Lecturer's Notebook

Shin Freedman

In the fall of 2016, I started my Fulbright experience in China. This was the result of years of planning, applications filled, and various other preparations. Actually, it was the realization of becoming a Fulbright scholar. I had first come in contact with the Fulbright Program in Korea. I was so impressed with the contact I had with Fulbright scholars that I thought I would like to become one someday.

Some things are simply unknowable, no matter how much you have prepared. There would be challenges as we embarked on our new and uncharted journey. My Fulbright colleague had warned me that the most important things happen with the host institution prior to arrival. I was not ready to absorb the full meaning of that advice until I received a rather perplexing email from my host university.

Toward the end of our week-long orientation in Beijing after our arrival in China, Fulbrighters were prepped to meet with our respective international relations staff, *waiban*, and get to know them, since on the last day we would travel together with our *waiban* to our host university. Zhejiang University (often referred to as Zheda, a short form of the Chinese name, Zhejiang Daxue), my host university, sent a teaching assistant instead. I wondered why my *waiban* was not present, as was the case with the other host universities. It was too early for me to learn how crucial it was for me to be open-minded and flexible as I adjusted to my new environment. Be like water![1]

I had arrived in China in the fall of 2016 as a Fulbright scholar with a set of preconceived notions that I would have the best time of my life as a teacher, love every aspect of living abroad in Hangzhou for the next five months, and solve whatever challenges I might encounter with the help of the Fulbright Commission, the Department of State, and local Beijing embassy staff. My husband, Jim, accompanied me to China. We are both experienced global travelers and particularly interested in Asia lately, in part because of Asia's soft intellectual power and increasing economic power.

Having Korean heritage and looking just like the Chinese but with limited functional Chinese language ability, I found that the experience of my daily life would depend entirely upon with whom and where I interacted: on campus vs. off campus, English-speakers vs. non-English speakers.

I was excited and anxiously waiting to arrive in China after the end of the 2016 G20 Summit in Hangzhou, my new home. Hangzhou was beautiful, having undergone numerous urban beautification projects in preparation for the first G20 Summit ever to be hosted by the PRC. Local people talked about how much cleaner the air was since the G20 leaders' visit to China; factories had been ordered to close, and workers were ordered to leave the city to ease the normally heavy traffic.[2] Hangzhou is famous for its history, West Lake (a UNESCO World Heritage Site), the longest man-made canal in the world, Dragon Well Tea (*Longjingcha*), and innovations such as being the home of Alibaba's mega online enterprise.

I had written to my host faculty member at Zheda in early summer before my arrival, requesting what I thought to be basic information: the course catalog, the academic calendar, and the department information, which I was not able to find on Zheda's English webpages. I did not get any response. Then, I attempted to connect with her by phone, and this too was unsuccessful.

My host faculty wrote to me that my role at the host institution would be as her teaching assistant. Though it was not clear where this misunderstanding had originated, I was quite shocked and perplexed by the rather arbitrary role assignment. A US Fulbright scholar acting as a teaching assistant at a host university? I politely and thoughtfully wrote back for clarification, citing the core mission of the Fulbright Scholar Program: "to increase mutual understanding through academic exchange."[3] After many more email exchanges during the summer, I started getting a different response. I was quite happy to learn from an affiliation letter that I would be given a teaching assistant, rather than play one. Puzzled by the earlier misunderstanding, I pondered its source: Was it because of the library and information science (LIS) discipline, my not having a doctoral degree as many of my Fulbright cohort had, or my direct manner of requesting what I needed from my host faculty? I would never know, but it became my ongoing research question while teaching my two courses: one seminar course titled Frameworks for Information Literacy for Higher Education and the other, Research Strategies and Practices. My Fulbright letter specified that I was to teach two graduate courses in the Information Resources Department, School of Public Affairs (SPA), at Zheda, which is ranked among China's top ten universities.

Thinking back, I should have copied the first rude email to all parties involved in the US-China Fulbright Program and at the host university. But alas, I did not pursue that route. Instead, I answered the best way I could on my own, independently. I did not share this unpleasant correspondence with anyone. That was my big mistake. I learned later from the Fulbright Program staff that I should always copy my emails to as many people as possible. When my counterpart asserted that she would supervise my class, I asked innocently, "Is this a common practice in Chinese universities?" Then, I explained how an American university would interpret the situation, and I never got any reply. There seemed to be so many of these situations— some nagging, some laughable, and some silly things that happened during my most interesting teaching experience.

Waiban, Administrator, and Faculty Colleagues

I had a rough start during my first week in Hangzhou. The apartment we were first taken to was unlike anything I had seen in the pictures. Dust, dead bugs, loose screen windows, and bare, unmade beds gave us the idea that the apartment had not been lived in for some time. The bathroom faucet gushed brown water. Though tired and wanting to go to bed early after a long trip, I hesitated to unpack my bags. When I asked my *waiban* about the apartment, she answered that due to the G20 Summit preparation, all the resources had been expended elsewhere so it had not been properly prepared. We spent the next four days at a hotel waiting for more suitable housing. I did not sleep well on the first night in Hangzhou, wondering if it would be like this for the rest of the semester. Surprisingly, my *waiban* seemed unconcerned about the condition of the apartment.[4] While our luggage was still unpacked in a hotel, an invitation for a meeting with the dean of the School of Public Affairs (SPA) came. On the fifth day, new living arrangements were eventually made with an apartment on the Zijinggang campus, where my classroom and my faculty colleagues would be. My husband was as relieved as I was to finally settle into our new place on campus.

The dean greeted us in a large official conference room at the new campus. We all formally shook hands. Then we proceeded with the gift exchange. I realized at that moment I did not bring gifts for everyone present. It was a mistake. Chinese culture takes gift giving seriously. At the Fulbright Orientation in DC, cultural affairs staff from the embassy in Beijing and Fulbright-China alumni had suggested that we bring gifts for university staff and faculty. In the Chinese context, gift giving is an expected behavior to show respect to another person and strengthen relationships.[5]

My host faculty stopped by to take me to lunch. She was apologetic about her spoken English, though I did not detect any problem. In person, I liked her right away. Apparently, I was one of the few Americans she had ever met in her life. Besides, I learned that I was the very first Fulbright scholar in the department and to the SPA. The Information Resource Management Department was the newest, one of the seven departments of the SPA. My relationship with department colleagues was rather random in part because of our different teaching schedules. My classes were held from early morning to noon; my Chinese colleagues' classes were usually in the late afternoon to evening. I patiently waited for a department meeting invitation. I had the distinct impression that only a few of my colleagues were proficient in oral English. That explained in part why some were rather shy at meeting me in person. Other than my host faculty and an occasional encounter with my department chair, I met my other colleagues and administrators only at official functions like the semester-end department party.

Colleagues told me that Chinese faculty members do not socialize with their students—even with graduate and PhD students. When I asked my host faculty about student/faculty relationships in China, she told me that she got invitations from the students, but she did not accept them. I concluded that Chinese teacher-and-student relationships were rather formal and socialization among them was a foreign concept. I realized how different this Chinese social norm was from that of Americans. Borrego asserts that all elements of academic environments form a learning community. While the classroom learning in a formal setting for a prescribed curriculum is important, informal learning occurs outside of the classroom through interactions with faculty members and other college personnel. Thus, an integrated learning environment can be more impactful for student learning.[6]

Halloween Party in China

My class had been going well, and the students were very diligent in their studies, so I decided to have a party, as a reward, in my apartment and invite all my students. The party theme was Halloween and included a potluck meal. They were excited about the upcoming party. A party committee was formed to coordinate the decoration, food preparation, and organization. A "potluck party" concept was of great interest to my students in a culture where the host usually provides everything. I provided the main dish, and the students brought their favorite snacks and party wares. Their costumes were scary and fun-loving and included one student dressed as Mr. Spock with Vulcan ears and a cloak and a girl in a sailor outfit. They all painted their faces with scary makeup just as we would during Halloween in the States. We also played games and read Edgar Allan Poe's "The Raven." Hearing Michael Jackson's "Thriller" in the background, everyone had a great time without disturbing any neighbors. The students left our apartment at nearly 11:00 p.m., almost three hours later than originally planned. Being responsible students, some stayed to help to clean up the tables, take down all decorations, and pack all trash. Everyone at the party was satisfied—taking many photos with Halloween costumes and busily uploading them to WeChat. We were pleased also.

On the following Monday, after a pleasant cultural exchange evening, I received an unexpected call from our US Embassy contact about "The Party" with my students. "Yes, we had fun—a real American experience," I answered.

She asked, "So . . . I heard you had the party with students' money?"

As I answered her questions, it suddenly occurred to me that the call was not about the success of the party but a possible complaint. This conversation took place on Monday afternoon, and the Halloween party had just been over the weekend. Someone had reported back to the Beijing-based Fulbright administration. I was shocked, to say the least. I explained that the students were supposed to bring the receipts back to me, and I was going to pay for the party preparation fees that the planning committee of four students had incurred.

She seemed to understand at that point, replying, "Oh, I thought the party happened some time ago."

The incident made me realize what this *waiban*'s function really was. From then on, I limited contact with my *waiban*, if I could. Jim and I managed to take care of all official travel matters on our own. This included booking our own trips, buying train tickets, picking up tickets, and reserving taxis to the train station for upcoming lecture invitations at cities outside Hangzhou. Unlike the locals, we had to pay extra fees to book the tickets online and pick them up. These extra fees were, as we understood, because we used a foreign credit card.

My expectations about my relationship with my *waiban* had gone awry, and the reality I faced was difficult. I was reminded of the first encounter with my *waiban* not being present at the Beijing Embassy Orientation to greet and accompany me to the host university, my delayed settling into suitable housing until the day classes started, and that not a single other Fulbright scholar had been invited to Zheda despite repeated conversations about the opportunities available. I was quite concerned about the situation and requested that the Fulbright staff visit our campus in the hopes that their help might improve the situation.

My Teaching Life

I had anticipated my teaching with excitement and some anxiety. I had diligently prepared for my two courses; yet I was concerned about my teaching style and whether the Chinese students would accept it easily. Moreover, I had a healthy dose of apprehension about the seminar course, as I had not yet taught this seminar in my home institution.

My graduate students were delightful in their devotion to studying and learning.[7] They, like all the students in Zheda, had been chosen in a competitive process from the national testing pool. Arriving early in the morning for my class, I noticed that my teaching assistant had placed a cup of hot tea on my table. A box of tissues was on the side near where I placed my laptop. At the slightest hint that technical assistance might be needed in viewing my lecture PowerPoints, three or more students would jump right in to help me. Whenever my students saw me on campus, they would take my bag and carry it for me. This respectful attention would be highly unusual in the US, but it was common practice there, given my age and position as a Fulbright scholar. During my lectures, students were attentive, respectfully taking notes and recording my lectures almost verbatim. However, when the discussions started, they were hesitant, not because the instructional language was in their second language of English (all my graduate students were quite proficient in spoken English and excellent in written English), but because they were unaccustomed to taking the risk of expressing their individual opinions openly for fear of contradicting their classmates or the professor's point of view.[8]

In each classroom activity, I organized students into groups, either in a mixed level of ability or in a mix of their academic-year ranking. Initially, the group activities in the class were received with reluctance. As I continually emphasized the value of "working together" in discussion and research projects, my students seemed to get the hang of it. After introducing "concept mapping" for research topic selection, one student told me that, "I have never considered applying [concept mapping] to research. . . . It broadened my horizon and improved my skills in research." And so, I realized that my students were familiar with the concepts but just had no experience in applying them. During class discussions on "Intellectual Property and Copyrights,"[9] one student expressed indignation at my demand to use international standards of scholarship and research. In fact, another asked point-blank, "Why should Chinese intellectuals follow the American standards of publishing guidelines when the Chinese standards are as good as any?" Taking this as a teachable moment, I introduced critical thinking and evaluation to continue this active discussion.

As the semester progressed, the students became not only more participative but delightfully outspoken in English and occasionally in Chinese, switching back and forth. I often rewarded them with clear, encouraging verbal praise, "That's a great question!" or a "high five."[10] This open praise was also something quite outside their comfort zone, and it took them a while to get used to it. On one occasion, one student did such a good job that I gave her a hug spontaneously. After a while, other students earned a hug and waited patiently for their reward. After the final class of the semester, my students lined up and would not let me leave until they had received their well-deserved reward—a hug. I took this as a clear sign that they had gotten the message that I wanted them to take responsibility for their learning.

Aside from teaching, the Fulbright Guest Lecture Program was a personally rewarding and professionally enhancing experience. Fulbright administrators brought together a list of lecture topics and shared the list with selected Chinese universities early in the fall. I started getting invitations from various universities across the country. The host institutions put us up at university hotels and also assisted us by sending students to greet us at railway stations. At other times, a *waiban* or host faculty with a university car would be waiting for us at the airport. They were great interpreters and companions who seemed to genuinely enjoy the direct contact with visiting lecturers like us.

The lecture circuit gave me the chance to talk about my research. In particular, the Beijing Institute of Technology (BIT) and Shanghai Normal University (SNU) organized conferences where I was a keynote speaker. At BIT, I spoke to an audience of university librarians from eleven universities around Beijing about the professional identity of academic librarians in the US. A lively Q&A followed, facilitated in Chinese and English. At SNU, my lecture was coordinated with the First International Conference on Republican Period Literature. The SNU faculty members invited me to the Chinese Comfort Women exhibit in the library. I was very touched by this tragic history.

My lecture at BIT happened to be on the morning of the US Thanksgiving Day, which I had forgotten when I accepted the invitation. After the lecture, there was a luncheon banquet where university staff and administrators treated us with gracious Chinese charm. Later that day, the dean invited us *again* to a dinner party in the city. After learning that we had missed our American Thanksgiving dinner, he included Beijing roast duck in place of turkey. We appreciated the spirit and hospitality of our BIT and SNU hosts. The next morning, we left for another lecture invitation from the School of Business and Management at Southwest University in Chongqing.

Daily Life

My daily life on campus began with visiting the main dining hall. From there, I took the campus shuttle or rode my one-speed bike to my office in the SPA building. Riding a bike in the corridors felt like a childlike pleasure that I had forgotten in the US. After teaching for four hours, I came back to my office to meet students or review materials for the next class until 5:00 p.m.; then, I was off to an off-campus fitness center by one-speed bike before having dinner at the main school dining hall with students, faculty, and staff. Riding a bike with the sea of students on bikes during campus rush hours was a unique experience.

Throughout my sojourn, Chinese language played a major part in our daily life, particularly off-campus. Unlike some of my Fulbright cohorts, I had a limited, elementary-level Chinese language proficiency. People spoke to me in rapid-fire colloquial tones as if I might understand. I usually deferred to Jim because he had enrolled in the intensive Chinese language course on campus, and I often relied on his spoken language ability. Funded by the Fulbright Program, I took Chinese language lessons for five months.

Making myself understood was one of the first problems I had to deal with. My Chinese tutor, Rachel, and I started lessons in my office. Rachel was an experienced Chinese language teacher who was very generous with her time. On the second week of our lessons, she invited us to the Mid-Autumn Festival dinner at her house. We met four people, including her son, husband, and her parents, who all lived in a rather tight space. Rachel's parents greeted us with a big smile and encouraged us to sample home-made pork dumplings and other dinner dishes. We were pleased to be invited to dine with a Chinese family on a Chinese holiday. I realized it was a special indicator of deep acceptance to be part of this dinner. Their house was one-third the size of my apartment, yet they seemed to be genuinely comfortable and accommodating as a family unit. Contrastingly, the American family structure rarely includes aging parents as part of their family whether one has adequate living space or not. It was endearing to be with them at the dinner that night, and the dumplings made by Rachel's father were delicious.

Rachel was curious and observant about every aspect of my life as a "foreign expert." Once, as we were about to start our language class, I got a call from Jim. As we were about to resume our Chinese language class, Rachel told me in amazement, "I have never said to my husband, 'I am sorry,' in our daily conversation." She further commented about how different it was to learn how American married couples talk to each other. "We, Chinese, don't talk like that!" She seemed to acknowledge that apology might be appropriate among close relationships. Apparently, it was Rachel's first time to hear any dialogue in the context of an apology. Since then, I shared with Rachel more about my life lessons – not because I am an expert but because Rachel reminded me of my younger self. In return, Rachel was especially willing to help me navigate and negotiate my daily encounters within the labyrinths of Chinese culture.

On weekends, we visited many local museums, parks, and canals together with Rachel's son, Daniel, and her husband, Eric. I invited Rachel to accompany me to a beauty parlor, as we both wanted to do something fun—a makeover of our looks. She eagerly accepted my suggestion. After that, we planned more trips and traveled to an ancient water town, Wuzhen, where her friend, a local businesswoman, had purchased a number of hotels, restaurants, and coffee shops in the past three years. Rachel's friend drove her luxury foreign car and guided us through the town, and we stayed at her hotel free of charge, enjoying free meals and coffee because we were her guests. It seems that young and successful entrepreneurs abound and are rapidly increasing in twenty-first-century China.[11]

In our daily lives, amenities taken for granted in the US, such as safe drinking water and hot water in public toilets for hand washing, were not available in Hangzhou. While we had to purchase filtered water for drinking, washing, and cooking, there were plenty of other benefits that would offset our perceived imbalance of basic needs. It was all about the people who bridged the cultural gulf we encountered. My students were always available to order our lunch at their favorite restaurants and have it delivered to our classroom or order items large or small through *Taobao* whenever we needed something.[12] Once I reached out for help from a total stranger because my ATM debit card was taken by the machine. This graduate student rescheduled her own doctor's appointment to accompany me to the bank to explain what had happened to my ATM card at the kiosk. A Chinese-American couple we met at the entrance of our apartment tower invited us to their living room when we unwittingly locked ourselves out one evening. On another occasion, a young cashier at a noodle shop near the gym we visited off-campus offered us a handwritten menu in English so that we knew what to order. We were impressed and satisfied by this simple gesture by ordinary folks in China.

At the Beijing airport on our last day, a check-in clerk stepped out from the counter with a serious look. As he escorted us to an immigration official, we were told, "Madam, your visa expired—two weeks ago." I could not believe what I just heard. How was it possible that my visa had expired while my husband's visa would not expire for two more weeks? I pleaded, "My *waiban* handled my residence visa application, as I am a Fulbright scholar at Zheda." I was terrified that we might miss our flight. I called the US Embassy for help and was told that I shouldn't worry, but how could I not? After waiting for over an hour and signing a letter explaining how my visa had expired, finally I was on my way home.

Conclusions and Reflections

By the time this book is published, it will be over two years since my Fulbright sojourn. Why did I initiate this edited volume of Fulbright lecturers' experiences? Why did I write my chapter? It came out of an inner discomfort about some aspects of my Fulbright experience. Curiously, I could not help feeling discomfort, yet, at the same time, satisfaction. It's a contradiction. My library and information science (LIS) teaching experience with bright Chinese graduate students was great; however, I ran into many issues (e.g., housing, Fulbright scholar's role mix-ups from the host university, and my *waiban*'s subversive role) before I stood comfortably in the classroom and in front of lecturing podiums in many Chinese universities. I pondered whether my Fulbright colleagues had similar experiences or whether, perhaps, they may not have had any discomfort at all with their distinguished credentials, fluent Chinese language ability, and teaching experience. In my case, the use of narrative inquiries helped me figure out how to "flow like water" in China. My one semester sojourn in China was a period of time when I experimented with my teaching and theoretical practices within a new framework and explored their potential for LIS education.

How did the misunderstanding happen before I arrived in Hangzhou, China? Had the Fulbright Program staff not informed my host university about what the role of a Fulbright scholar should be? Had the misunderstanding happened because of political differences, language limitations, or cultural differences across two countries? My own psychosocial development has expanded dramatically from the Fulbright experience, including an expanded geopolitical awareness, cross-cultural sensitivity, and an awareness of the demand for global higher education. In my own discipline of library and information science, I am even more aware of how much access to information matters. My Americanism demanded the information I needed, whereas my host university may have seen it in an entirely different light, asking, "Who is this person asking for so much information?" and responding with silence. This American responded in a louder voice: "Have you not received my email? Answer me."

When I met my host faculty face-to-face, all my earlier miscommunications disappeared. We apologized to each other for our lack of fluency in the other's language. We recognized and respected each other, having acknowledged that hosting a Fulbright scholar was a new experience for them, as well as for me as a Fulbright lecturer. We had a lot to learn from each other. My Chinese graduate students asked me to come back to attend many important events in their lives, such as graduation and foreseeable wedding ceremonies. I felt great connection receiving these invitations. Perhaps I would not have felt such deep satisfaction without first having encountered discomfort. Having tackled challenging issues earlier helped me see the brighter path at the end.

At the end of the semester, my host faculty proposed to do research collaboratively. I was taken aback. Suddenly forgetting all about our earlier tensions and my own skepticism, I was delighted beyond description by this changed, more positive attitude. She also shared that the department's future plan was to integrate Archive Management and Information Resources Management into one unit, as I had discussed on several occasions, drawing from the current practice and trends in American LIS. For the first time, I felt that my Fulbright presence had made a difference at the department curricular level and that the LIS contents and material might impact our research collaboration. I recognized and experienced a shift in perception and professional acceptance by my Chinese colleagues despite the times when I felt troubled and disconnected but had been unable to articulate those feelings.

As a major snowstorm welcomed us back to Boston, I had two snow days to contemplate the meaning of my Fulbright experience and beyond. I thought about whether I had made any real difference in the education of my Chinese students. They were still on the Spring Festival holiday—*Chunjie* vacation. As I reviewed the assessment survey results for the semester evaluation, the students clearly articulated what they had learned. I felt a deep sense of satisfaction about the five months I had spent, and I was eager to see my former Chinese students join me in the professional world of LIS on a global scale. My Fulbright experience had given me confidence in my teaching and confirmed why I wanted to be an educator in the first place. After all, being part of the global Fulbright educational exchange was something really special.

Notes

1. Water is fluid, soft, and yielding, but water will wear away rock which is rigid and cannot yield (Lao Tzu). See also Alan Watts, *Tao: The Watercourse Way* (New York: Penguin Books, 1977). Print.
2. *The Guardian*, August 30, 2016, and *The China Daily*, September 5, 2016, reports on the Group of 20 Summit in Hangzhou. Print.
3. Per Fulbright Scholar Program website, "Core Fulbright U.S. Scholar Program." Web. December 18, 2018.
4. A typical dormitory for graduate students has three students in one room. Other Chinese universities may differ in the number of students in one room with as many as four for graduate students, which I learned from personal communications with students I met at my school and other universities during my lecture circuit.
5. Paul Steidlmeirer, "Gift Giving, Bribery and Corruption: Ethical Management of Business Relationships in China," *Journal of Business Ethics* 20 (1999): 121–132. Print.
6. Susan E. Borrego, "Mapping the Learning Environment," in *Learning Reconsidered 2: A Practical Guide to Implementing a Campus-Wide Focus on the Student Experience*, ed. R.P. Keeling (Washington, DC: National Association of Student Personnel Administrators, American College Personnel Association, 2006), 11–16. Print.
7. In my home institution, the majority of the graduate students have jobs, are married, and study part-time; however, the Chinese graduate students study full-time, and all my students were unmarried and lived in campus dormitories.

8. Helena Hing Wa Sit, "Characteristics of Chinese Students' Learning Styles," *International Proceedings of Economics Development and Research* 62 (2013): 36. Print.

9. There was a landmark case won by a former basketball star, Michael Jordan, who finally won an intellectual property case against the Chinese Sporting Company's copyright infringement, which had been lost in two previous cases. The verdict, from the Supreme People's Court, reversed previous rulings by lower courts in Beijing that said Qiaodan, based in the southern province of Fujian, could use the Chinese characters for Jordan to sell their goods. Then the Chinese Supreme Court finally admitted the wrongdoing of copying the trademark of Michael Jordan. I used this current court case ruling as an example of our discussion to elicit students' reactions in December 2016.

10. My students wrote in their reflective journals that my teaching style emphasized more on action, as opposed to that of the Chinese faculty, who educated through words. Upon my return to my home university in the US, my Chinese students wrote to me, specifically: "Writing reflective journals is the teaching method I remember most, for this enables us to review what we've learned in the class and thus we could listen to the class more attentively. In your classes, you tended to pay more attention to our progress over time and the ability to work as a team. In other classes, professors focus more on the work and results, and we often do research on our own."

11. Personal conversation took place with Rachel's friend who was a housewife only three years ago but who now owns one-third of the hotels and restaurants in Wuzhen. For a description of this new generation of China's entrepreneurs, see "The Rise of Entrepreneurship in China," *Forbes*, April 2016. Print.

12. Since we did not have a Chinese bank account, we were not able to use either the Taobao (online shopping system) or the Didi system.

5 This Too Is China

Hui Muslim Culture and the Fulbright Experience at Ningxia University

Pat Munday

Framed by narrative inquiry with its emphasis on temporality, sociality, and place,[1] this is the story of my one-semester Fulbright in Yinchuan, a city in the rather remote province of Ningxia in northwest China. After nearly thirty years at my home university, it was easy to forget how much I loved teaching and why I had entered the profession. Gone were the many duties and distractions that fill the days at my home university in Montana. Teaching only two classes instead of my usual three or four allowed generous time for class preparation and interaction with students and colleagues. As an American professor in an out-of-the-way province, I was recognizable and popular. Students of all stripes introduced themselves to me in the dining halls or other places, and many informally attended my lectures. Traditional Confucian values are still woven deeply into Chinese culture, and with that tradition comes a profound respect for teachers. Foreign teachers, especially, are held in high regard and treated like honored guests.

Daily Life

Daily life at Ningxia University (Ningda, the suffix "da" means "big") was idyllic. My routine demonstrates the role of temporality as a fundamental organizing approach to narrative inquiry.[2] Classes in solid blocks of time on Tuesday and Thursday evenings left long weekends for adventures into the remote Ningxia countryside and for guest lectures at other Chinese universities. The atmosphere in my workplace at the postgraduate office was hours of quiet alternating with light conversation, consultations with young colleagues about their students' research papers, group lunches at a nearby dining hall, and snack-sharing time in the morning and afternoon. My interest in traditional Chinese foodways and the notion of food-as-medicine helped structure many conversations. My apartment was on the eleventh floor of a new faculty/staff apartment tower. Because it was a new building and did not yet have Wi-Fi, I worked almost daily—including weekends—at my desk in the postgraduate office, a twenty-minute walk from my apartment. Several paths wound their way along a small lake, and the adjoining park was beautifully landscaped in a way that made it seem natural. It was as if Frederick Law Olmsted, the designer of many delightful urban park spaces in America, had designed the Ningda campus. There was even a perfect rock to climb for morning yoga—a carefully arranged formation with a tall central scholar rock (gongshi, 供石) surrounded by a spiral of what seemed to be student rocks. It was a place where powerful natural spirits called *shén* (上帝) might reside.[3] Indeed, the space of this park, as well as my workspace, came to play an important role in how I interacted with students and colleagues.[4]

Strolling along the campus lake on the path to my apartment, I observed a young man—a senior engineering student, as it turned out—practicing archery in the park. He committed many errors, ranging from inconsistent anchor (the place on your face where your hand draws the arrow) to a wild release (the hand letting loose the arrow) like a folk musician plucking a string bass. Concerned at my observing him, he asked in very good English, "Is something wrong, sir?"

I introduced myself, explained that I had practiced archery for many years, and asked if he would like some instruction. Bowen[5] was a quick study and within two weeks was shooting very well, given that his bow and arrows cost less than 100 yuan (about $15) from the popular Internet shopping site Alibaba. One day, I returned from class to find Bowen sitting on the steps of my apartment tower, a package in his arms.

"Master," he addressed me, "I have been waiting for you."

"Bowen," I asked, "why didn't you just text me to find out when I would return?"

"Oh, Master, I knew you would come home."

With two hands, he offered me the package, which I opened to find a bow and arrows like his.

"A gift for you, Master."

After this, we practiced archery and shared a dinner each week. I told him stories about hunting and life in Montana; he told me stories about his engineering education and his father's battle with cancer. After graduation, he returned home to care for his father and took a part-time job at a neighborhood business. When I asked about his engineering career, he explained with wet eyes that his career could wait until he was finished caring for his father. Loyalty to and sacrifice for family are just one of the many profound lessons that I learned from my Chinese students.

Teaching

In each of my two classes, a student volunteered as my teaching assistant. In China, class monitors are chosen from the primary grades on, and by the time they get to college, these students are experienced and efficient at leading and organizing their fellow students.[6] At my home university, it usually takes several meetings and a number of emails with a graduate teaching assistant to complete routine tasks, such as setting up the class roll and a website for distributing class materials. Within an hour—and with no help or supervision from me—the class monitors had set up a WeChat (the Facebook-like Chinese social media app) group, distributed the syllabus/schedule and reading materials, and created a calendar to remind students when assignments were due. I also asked my teaching assistants to arrange weekly meals with a small group of students from each class. Meals are central to social bonding and group cohesiveness in China, a milieu in which stories unfold and academics is invested with personal meaning. At twice-a-week meals, I personally got to know my students, they practiced English, and we explored our mutual curiosity about one another's culture. The meal typically cost less than 200 yuan (about 30 dollars) for six people. With students choosing the restaurant, I enjoyed a wide variety of meals from the dozens of dining places that surrounded the campus. The temporal structure of this Fulbright experience was very different from the rush of days at my home university. After meals or evening events, such as performances at the music college, we sometimes visited the night market outside one of the university gates. Dozens of vendors sold clothing, crafts, fresh produce, and street foods, such as roasted sweet potatoes and spicy lamb kabobs. On warm evenings, the night market was a friendly mob of students, families, retirees, beggars, and merchants—and another happy memory of my time in China.

In American universities, we see the best and brightest of Chinese students, highly self-selected on the basis of confidence and eagerness to travel abroad. In my previous experiences at Chinese universities, I had encountered only elite upper-division students. Because at Ningda I was assigned classes with first-year and sophomore students, I saw a new side of Chinese higher education. Students struggled to meet the onerous demands of taking eight to ten classes each semester, many of which required extensive memorization and recitation. Students were also expected to participate in extracurricular activities, such as speech and debate and dance and musical performances. Ningda offered many study abroad opportunities—especially with the University of Dubai and Missouri State University. The competition to be admitted to these programs was intense, though some students feared being away from home for a semester or longer.

My Ningda students reminded me of how much I take for granted about what American students know when they begin my classes. As an important lesson in temporality, I slowed down in lectures and discussions, covered much less material, and incorporated more examples. Expecting to teach upper-division students, I had planned a mid-semester research proposal and lengthy final research paper. My teaching assistants explained that students were terrified and would be incapable of either the level of research (five journal articles and two books) or the lengthy paper. I agreed to require a proposal based on a single primary document and a final essay of just a few hundred words.

Relief from the tedium of college committees allowed me time to interact with faculty colleagues. With them, I enjoyed restaurant meals and field trips to local sites. My office location, a desk in the postgraduate teaching office, furthered sociality. After some reflection, the dean thought this too humble a station and generously offered me a shared office with a visiting Korean professor. I politely declined. Daily office life with the master's-level postgraduates who were teaching and performing administrative functions allowed me to learn much more about Chinese culture and higher education—and how Chinese colleagues construct identity through social interactions—than I could have learned sitting in a semi-private office with another foreigner. The five postgraduates—one man and four women—in my office were a lively bunch, all about 30 years old and with the many hopes and fears that attend that uncertain stage in life. One was married with a bright, beautiful 2-year-old who took to me like her adopted grandpa; the others were in various relationships that they were very secretive about despite or perhaps because of the frequent gossip.

I became good friends with Matthew, a young male teacher. He was the first more-or-less openly gay man that I had met in China, which for him brought on a host of anxieties driven by the deeply prejudicial social mores against LGBT relationships in China. Matthew was a devout Christian, had lived and worked in the US, and had excellent English. As my friend and confidant, and as two men, we had frank discussions about sexuality in China vs. the US, as well as academic discussions about research questions he was considering before committing to a doctoral program. Although his instructor-level position was considered more or less permanent, he feared a national and provincial push to raise faculty standards, with the PhD becoming a necessary qualification. We also discussed religious issues.

The Hui Minority

In previous visits to China, I learned about common stereotypes regarding minorities. As a Uighur Muslim friend and former student phrased it,

"China loves its minorities—so long as they are dressed in costume—old men playing music or young women dancing." I liked my Uighur students from a previous teaching stint in China and became (and remain) good friends with one.[7] Uighurs—Caucasian Chinese people from the northwest province of Xinjiang—have a troubled history with the central government, and the Uighur nationalist movement has resulted in sometimes harsh government reprisals and restrictions. The Uighur students generally resented and feared the central government, and most of the Han Chinese students nursed various prejudices and stereotypes about Uighurs. One dinner erupted into a loud argument when two female Han students questioned the three male Uighurs about their refusal to eat pork. This escalated into the women accusing the men of being ungrateful for the special minority privileges granted to them. Other Han students warned me that "Uighurs all carry knives" and were dangerous and that I must be careful.

Naively, I thought the situation with Hui Muslim students in Ningxia province would be similar and was initially surprised that Fulbright allowed a placement there. My naïve assumptions were false and helped force me to be more sensitive and attuned to Hui ethnography. In my first weeks on campus, I saw few outward signs of Hui culture. The school dining halls and most off-campus restaurants were Halal, as marked with bilingual Chinese/Arabic signs. Of my seventy-three students, about thirty-five were Muslim females, and of these, only three wore the hijab. My Hui students seemed no more or less conservative than the Han in how they dressed or behaved. As I learned, however, the social dimensions of Hui Muslim culture are complicated and diverse when it comes to marriage, employment prospects, foodways, rural poverty, and education.

Hui Muslims have been part of the Middle Kingdom since Islam came to northwest China via the Silk Road in the seventh century.[8] Because Yinchuan was a major stop on the Silk Road and for various other historical reasons[9]—including the Mongolian emperors' (Yuan Dynasty) favored treatment of Hui over Han people[10]—Hui Muslims became the dominant population in what is now Ningxia. In China overall, Hui are the largest of several Muslim minorities. Though Hui constitute less than 1% of China's total population, in the Ningxia Hui Autonomous Region, they represent about 40% of the total, and Hui are the majority in some counties.

Hui is an ethnic category loosely based on legendary descent from Arabs or Persians. On the one hand, Hui is a self-assigned identity reinforced by Islamic religious practices, family influence when choosing marriage partners, and foodways. On the other hand, Hui is a formal Chinese government minority designation recorded on one's identification card, which affords benefits similar to US affirmative action programs. For example, Hui and other minorities were exempt from the former one-child policy, and Hui and other minority high-school graduates receive bonus points on the *gaokao* (National Higher Education Entrance Examination). As Gladney concludes, Hui culture is best seen as a social negotiation or "dialogical interaction" between self-identification and government-imposed identity and is in constant flux.[11]

In contemporary China, Hui Muslims occupy a crucial niche in China's foreign trade strategy, with Yinchuan a hub for Arab trade. The first China-Arab States Expo opened there in 2013 and is now an annual event. Tourism, educational exchanges, and other cultural activities (i.e., soft diplomacy) are central to China's efforts to establish relationships with Arab states. The Chinese government is building a fantastic Global Muslim City at a cost of nearly $4 billion in Yinchuan, replete with a Hui Culture Park and Taj Mahal-like entrance.[12] Also in Yinchuan, I visited a shiny new Arab trade center with business offices and a large open-air mall with fountains and Islamic sculptures.[13]

Narrative Inquiry with Hui Students

To help me understand Hui culture, students organized small group discussions at the campus tea house.[14] Like group meals at restaurants, tea proved to be a special time and safe space for the unfolding of a unique narrative. All the discussion participants were women, although I talked individually with a few male Hui students.[15] On one occasion, a non-Hui woman joined the group. Her roommate Cheryl, a Hui student in the group, encouraged her to learn more about why she was awakened by her roommate's prayers and meals in the pre-dawn hours during the holy month of Ramadan.

Cheryl was among the more devout of my Hui students. She wore the hijab to pray although she did not wear it to classes. She and the other Hui students explained that the hijab was a personal choice,[16] although many said they wore it at home out of respect for parents and grandparents. Also, they explained, once married, they planned to wear the hijab in their daily life.

Many female Hui students at Ningda were self-selected as daughters of parents who valued education and did not encourage early marriage. This represented a new generational attitude and opportunity, since many of their mothers and aunts had little or no formal education. This was in part social because of historical bias against women's education and employment in Hui culture and in part economic because of required fees for public education. Public education is still limited for many rural students, who usually finish sixth grade but then often drop out because of lack of local access to or the need to pay fees for middle and high school. The government recognizes this "education gap" and invests heavily in rural school infrastructure and more highly qualified teachers.[17]

Colleagues told me that rural students receive an inferior education and, even if they attend college, will never close that gap. Karl, a non-Hui postgraduate, described to me his cousin who grew up in a large city and graduated with a teaching degree from a good university. The cousin was assigned to teach several years at a primary school in a remote, poor Hui town in southern Ningxia. Karl believed the mission had a reverse effect: instead of helping rural students achieve a higher educational level, the cousin returned to the city permanently corrupted by lax rural educational values. Karl even thought that his cousin's pronunciation and vocabulary of standard Mandarin Chinese was impaired. The solution, he explained, was for rural Chinese families to move to larger cities where they would have better economic opportunities and their children would have access to better schools. This is, in fact, the dominant pattern in China and one reinforced by government policies encouraging rural-to-urban migration.[18]

My Hui students from rural Ningxia or neighboring provinces described female classmates who married young (about age 15) and stayed at home from that time on. Children from poorer rural families might begin work in their family's business or farm at about age 5 and drop out of school after grade six. Students described their parents' generation as families typically with three to five children; in contrast, they generally aspired to have just two—one boy and one girl. They thought it acceptable to date Han boys but would marry only a Hui. However, they explained, boys could marry Han girls so long as the girl agreed to convert to Islam. Becoming Hui was easy, involving only a ceremony and an oath.

For my students, being Hui meant being Muslim. By far the most obvious marker for my question, "What does it mean to be Hui?" was refraining from eating pork and avoiding drinking tea or eating in a place that was non-pure (i.e., non-Halal).[19] This prohibition means that Hui must not eat in a place where pork is cooked and served, because pork contaminates the cooking vessels and tableware. For some Hui Muslims, "pure" (*Qingzhen*, 清真) has a fundamental spiritual meaning whereby a person who eats pork contaminates all dishes he or she eats or drinks from. Travel in China, where the dominant Han culture prefers pork over other meats, is challenging for observant Hui. Thus many carry their own food when traveling to Han places without *Qingzhen* restaurants. In *Qingzhen* restaurants in Yinchuan, mutton seemed to be the preferred meat and carried an almost holy (or mythic, in terms of narrative inquiry) connotation.[20] Though significantly more expensive than chicken or even beef, sheep are raised locally, and eating mutton seemed a celebration of Hui-ness. In a broader sense, the prohibition on eating pork means that Hui identity is performed each time Hui people choose and eat at a *Qingzhen* restaurant. My Han students and colleagues occasionally remarked on this, and while they honored the

Hui request to eat *Qingzhen* when dining in mixed groups (maintaining group harmony is a cherished Chinese value), they also sometimes found it "inconvenient" (a term frequently used to mean "denied of choice") and sometimes disparaged mutton.

In a more conservative sense, the hijab for women and skullcap (taqiyah) for men are also markers of Islam. On campus, few students wear these, but in the Hui neighborhood around the architecturally beautiful Nan Guan mosque in Yinchuan, hijabs and taqiyahs were common. Students said only men prayed at the mosque and were surprised to learn that mosques in other countries often have separate facilities for women's prayer. Similarly, only men were expected to pilgrimage to Mecca (the Hajj). Traditionally, older, retired men make the trip, but several of my students had brothers or uncles who had gone.

My Hui students emphasized great respect for their grandparents when it came to questions of culture and religion. On campus and when away from home, most were admittedly lax about food habits, fasting for Ramadan, prayers, and dress. However, they all described being observant when at home with family and when it came to major festivals or ceremonies, such as Ramadan (Eid Al Fitr), Eid al-Adha ("Feast of Sacrifice"), and funeral ceremonies. The meat consumed at these festivals or ceremonies (a sheep or goat might be slaughtered) gave deeply spiritual and mythic meaning to the event.

Dominant Han culture is rife with misunderstandings of Islamic culture and Hui people. Han students who attended K–12 schools in areas with few or no Hui people told me they were taught nothing about Islamic culture. Others had wild beliefs, and several students told me that swine are sacred to Muslims, which is why Hui do not eat pork.[21] As an American professor, I found this surprising, and it can be deeply insulting to Islamic people. Just as in America, there also seemed to be considerable resentment in dominant culture regarding affirmative action.[22]

Lydia, a graduate student, learned of my discussions with undergraduates and came to talk with me. As the only Hui graduate student in the program who wore the hijab, I had noticed her at a few guest lectures I delivered to graduate-level classes. She did not wear the hijab as an undergraduate, she explained, but had become increasingly interested in her religion during the past year or so. She read the Quran (in Mandarin Chinese, not Arabic), took some religious instruction from a female imam, and had many discussions about Islam with her friends and relatives. She was proud of Islam coming to China on the Silk Road, of her descent from Persian immigrants centuries ago, and of loan words that came into the local dialect from Persian and Arabic.

Lydia described her goal of marrying a devote Hui man, but—to my surprise (at which she laughed)—said she would happily marry a Han man if he would convert to Islam. She admitted that some families might not accept this but thought that hers would. She was convinced that as younger Hui age, they will begin to fear Allah, submit to Allah's will, and demonstrate their piety though religious observance. She also hopes to visit Mecca, though she thinks this unnecessary so long as she is pious on a day-to-day basis.

All in all, Lydia seemed a remarkable person, someone who combined her cultural and religious traditions with a thoroughly modern feminism. She had also heard about my interest in food and, smiling to see a bag of dried red dates on my desk, explained how this was the holy food of the Prophet Mohammed and the purest food for breaking the day's fast during Ramadan. She advised me to eat seven each day.[23] Lydia anticipated the end of Ramadan in the coming week. An imam would kill a sheep. It would be cooked with potatoes and served with a traditional kind of cake cooked in oil. On the side, there would be potato noodles served dry with beef or cooked wet (i.e., in soup) with mutton, along with cold dishes of carrots, peppers, and other vegetables. She emphasized the importance of impeccable hygiene to mark the end of Ramadan: one must shower, be clean, and wear fresh, clean clothes—new clothes if possible. Lydia explained that Ramadan was just one of the wonderful holidays that marked the Islamic year. Seventy days after Ramadan would come Eid-e-qurban (Aid-al-Adha in Arabic), a feast specially marked by the sacrifice of a calf or sheep, or—for wealthy families—a camel.

Rural Hui Life

Near the end of my Fulbright, I witnessed Hui hospitality and food practices firsthand. While teaching at ZhongShan (Sun Yat-sen) University in Guangzhou, I had become friends with geology professor Zhang Ke, or Kerry,[24] who had years of fieldwork in Ningxia. He and his wife came to see me for a geological and historical tour of the countryside. My former student, Huang Lu, or "Lu," works as a scientist in eastern China, and he visited at the same time. We then met up with Ma Zhangwu, Kerry's former student. Mr. Ma is a Hui person from southern Ningxia, and between his local knowledge and Kerry's fieldwork experience, we had an amazing tour.

The tour included a fault-line from the infamous 1920 (7.8 magnitude) Haiyuan earthquake that killed more than 200,000 people. We visited a dry streambed that had shifted tens of meters laterally, a large tree split as the fault shifted, and a now-abandoned village of adobe construction destroyed by the earthquake. In addition to his passion for geology, Kerry has a profound respect for the historical and cultural wealth of China. We visited portions of the rammed earth Great Wall (Ming Dynasty), the Tongxin

Buddhist-style Great Mosque (Ming Dynasty), and the Xumishan Buddhist grottoes (fourth through ninth centuries). There are 130 or more grottos—most severely disfigured by Red Guards during the Cultural Revolution (late 1960s). As we viewed an ancient but defaced black Buddha along the trail through this mountain pass on the Silk Road, a group of young Chinese men and women joined us. Kerry took this as an opportunity for an impromptu lecture, which he later translated for me. "Look!" he cried, pointing at the damaged carving. "*This* was the Cultural Revolution. This was Chinese people destroying their own precious cultural heritage."

We capped our rural tour with a visit to Mr. Ma's family. His mother and father greeted Kerry and his wife like the old friends they were and treated Lu and me to the precious hospitality that even the humblest rural Chinese are famous for. Mr. Ma was the first in the village to attend college, and to mark his graduation, the village had taken up donations for a bronze plaque commemorating this achievement. We arrived well before sunset during Ramadan. In anticipation of our visit, Mr. Ma's father had gone into the hills and killed a lamb, which the elder mother roasted for us as honored guests in her home. While we ate this magnificent feast, the family went out into the courtyard for the prayer at sunset that preceded their evening meal.

Conclusions and Reflections

From my Fulbright experience, I have a newfound appreciation for my American students. Though not so diligent or punctual as Chinese students, they actively engage with course material, participate in lively class discussion, and will critically challenge my ideas or explanations. Even most sophomore-level American students can pull together a reasonably good (and original) research proposal, and junior-level students are capable of interrogating scholarly articles and writing a critical literature review. Chinese higher education looks to American universities as a model for student-centered teaching and learning, critical scholarship, and creative research. Through social media, I have stayed in contact with many of my students from Ningxia, and some now study in the US. Many transcended their Confucian self-censorship, and we have had engaging discussions including President Xi's consolidation of power, China's One Belt, One Road initiative, and problems in American society. Still, I believe that given the Confucian traditions in education and the reluctance of Chinese college administrators to support academic freedom, Chinese universities will struggle to play a lead role in global higher education. Ongoing Internet censorship, such as blocking Google Scholar, makes it very difficult for Chinese researchers to find Western publications.

Teaching on a Fulbright in China was a grand academic and social adventure. I liked the Chinese colleagues and students I met on this and previous visits to China, and I remain fascinated by the nation's diverse geography and culture. Chinese students revere their teachers and are eager to learn more about American culture, which I enjoy teaching from a historical and environmental perspective. I wanted to live and teach at an inland university and to better understand a significant minority group that played a large role in Chinese history from the Silk Road to the present day. I achieved these goals and will forever treasure my friends from Ningda.

Shortly after coming home to Montana, I dropped my cell phone into the water while fly fishing on a local river. It was an older phone and should have been no great loss, but when I tried to migrate my WeChat account to a new phone, there was a problem. WeChat closed my account, and formal appeals went unanswered.[25] I lost contact with dozens of Chinese students and colleagues for whom I had no other contact information, and as I dealt with this loss and my grief-like feelings, I came to deeply appreciate how meaningful my Fulbright in China had been. Though I've been able to restore most contacts through my teaching and departmental email contacts, many of the students I met—such as my archery student, Bowen—remain lost to me.

Notes

1. For an excellent brief overview of narrative inquiry, see D. Jean Clandinin and Janice Huber, "Narrative inquiry," in *International Encyclopedia of Education*, 3rd ed, ed. B. McGaw, E. Baker, and P.P. Peterson (Elsevier, In Press). Web. 01 April 2018.
2. On the role of time, especially in narrative, see Donald E. Polkinghorne, *Narrative Knowing in the Human Sciences* (Albany: State University of New York, 1988), 131–135; and Clandinin & Huber, 3–4. Print.
3. Stephen Little, *Spirit Stones of China* (Berkeley: University of California Press, 1999). On spiritual beings, see Stephen F. Teiser, "The Spirits of Chinese Religion," in *Religions of China in Practice*, ed. Donald S. Lopez (Princeton, NJ: Princeton University Press, 1996), 3–37. Web. 15 November 2017.
4. On the importance of place in narrative inquiry, see the section on the Bay Street School in D. Jean Clandinin and F. Michael Connelly, *Narrative Inquiry: Experience and Story in Qualitative Research* (Hoboken, NJ: Wiley & Sons, 2000), 89–91. Print.
5. Most Chinese college students have an English name. This and all other names in this chapter, unless otherwise noted, are pseudonyms.
6. For a glimpse into the competitiveness of the monitor selection process, see the documentary film, Weijun Chen, dir., *Please Vote for Me*, DVD (San Francisco: Steps International, 2007). Print.
7. This was at Southwest University in Chongqing, where I taught a class of "pregraduate minority elite students"—a competitively selected group of minority students from all over China who received special preparation for graduate school.

8. On the role of the Silk Road in transforming Chinese culture, see Xinru Liu, "Silk Road Legacy: The Spread of Buddhism and Islam," *Journal of World History* 22 (2011): 55–81. Print. As a historical overview including the many mosques, Sufi-led movements, and political struggles of the Hui people, see Michael Dillon, *China's Muslim Hui Community: Migration, Settlement, and Sects* (Abingdon, UK: Routledge, 2015; first published by Curzon Press, 1999). Print.

9. Yinchuan was originally the capital of the Buddhist Western Shia Empire. Because the empire resisted Mongol rule, the Yuan Dynasty razed the city in 1227, and it was rebuilt and settled by Hui Muslims after this time.

10. The Mongol rulers implemented a four-class system, where Hui Muslims were in the second tier, just below the Mongols. Melanie Jones-Leaning and Douglas Pratt, "Islam in China: From Silk Road to Separatism," *The Muslim World* (2012): 308–334. Print. The first Mongol emperor, Genghis Khan, was not always so benevolent to Hui Muslims and forbade some Islamic practices, such as Halal slaughter.

11. Dru C. Gladney, *Muslim Chinese: Ethnic Nationalism in the People's Republic* (Cambridge, MA: Harvard University Press, 1996), 76–78, 299–302. Print.

12. Kyle Haddad-Fonda, "China's Massive, Garish Theme Park for the Muslim World," *Foreign Policy*, May 11, 2016. Web. 04 November 2017.

13. On China's efforts to build bilateral trade with Arab states, see Wai-Yip Ho, "Mobilizing the Muslim Minority for China's Development: Hui Muslims, Ethnic Relations, and Sino-Arab Connections," *Journal of Comparative Asian Development* 12, no. 1 (2013): 84–112. Print.

14. Hui Muslim culture in China is extremely diverse and a function of local identity. Studies show that Hui Muslim culture in Yunnan or Xi'an is very different from that in Ningxia. See Lesley Turnbull, "Localizing Transnationalism in Post-Reform China: Sino-Islamic Identities among Hui-Muslim Women in Yunnan," in *Hui Muslims in China*, ed. Gui Rong, Hacer Zekiye Gönül, and Zhang Xiaoyan (Belgium: Leuven University Press, 2016), 129–154. Print.; and Ayesha Qurrat Ul Ain, "Everyday Life of a Chinese Muslim: Between Religious Retention and Material Acculturation," *Journal for the Study of Religions and Ideologies* 14 (2015): 209–237. Print. Ul Ain's study focuses on Hui Muslims in Xi'an.

15. My students were overwhelmingly female. Of the seventy-three students in my two classes, only nine were male.

16. Some sources report that women wearing the hijab are sometimes publicly ridiculed or experience prejudicial treatment by Han people. See e.g., Kimberly Yam, "China Is Home to 23 Million Muslims: Here Is One Woman's Story," *Huffpost*, May 08, 2017. Web. November 10, 2017.

17. Xin Miao and Christina W.Y. Wong, "Teaching: China Is Closing Its Rural Education Gap," *Nature* 511, no. 7509 (2014): 292. Print.

18. Huafeng Zhang, "Opportunity or New Poverty Trap: Rural-Urban Education Disparity and Internal Migration in China," *China Economic Review* 44 (2017): 112–124. Print. How different this is from American culture, where people generally believe that urban K–12 schools are inferior to schools in smaller cities and towns.

19. "Pure" is a Hui adaptation of the Islamic concept of Halal, translated in Chinese as *Qingzhen*—literally "Purity and Truth." The Hui Muslim sense of *Qingzhen* extends well beyond Halal. See Ho (2013) and Liang Zhang, "Qingzhen: Embodiment of Islamic Knowledge and Lifestyle," in Rong, 155–175.

20. On myths having "a quasi-objective collective existence," per Levi-Strauss, see Polkinghorne, 82–83, 85–86.
21. This ignorance among the dominant Han culture seems prevalent. One researcher reported a common misconception from a Han informant: "I know that pigs are holy and respected by all people in Islam. Because of this they do not eat pork." In Frauke Drewes, "Being Chinese and Being Muslim: Portrayals of the Hui Minority by Muslims, Non-Muslims, and the Media," *Rong* (2016): 97–111, at p. 103. Print.
22. Given the minority designation on one's official identity card, to be Hui is a more rigid category than minority or religious self-identification in American culture.
23. I later researched the significance of eating seven each day and found it derives from traditional Hadiths (i.e., teachings from the Prophet). See Ibn Qay'em El-Jozeyah, *The Prophetic Medicine* (Egypt: Dar Al-Ghadd Al-Gadeed, 2003), trans. Abd El-Qader, 121, 123, 371, 438, 530. Web. 14 October 2018.
24. I have used real names for Zhang Ke, Huang Lu, and Ma Zhanwu.
25. The most plausible explanation I have heard is that my WeChat account was linked to my Chinese phone number. When I returned to the US, I did not change my account information, and after some fixed time, my Chinese number was deactivated, and thus my WeChat account could not be validated.

6 Learning to See

A Fulbright Semester Teaching Painting in Beijing

Amy Cheng

I

I spent the spring of 2017 as a visiting professor in the Graduate Painting Program at Renmin University of China in Beijing. I was born in Taiwan, immigrating to the West with my family at age 4. My parents grew up in China, and we spoke Chinese at home. But despite being ethnically Chinese, I experienced two cultural gaps while teaching in China, the first one in the student-teacher relationship and the second one on the subject matter of the course itself.

My Chinese students' ability to understand English varied widely, but they all had handy Chinese-to-English translation apps on their cell phones. I depended on my MacBook Air as an essential teaching tool, since my Chinese vocabulary is limited to the domestic and quotidian; I carried it with me everywhere and relied on Google Translate. I would type out entire paragraphs; if the translation came out garbled, they would let me know, and I would rephrase and try again. I made myself available once a week for studio visits with students not enrolled in my class; in this way, I was able to meet other art students, both graduate and undergraduate. I also took interested students on field trips to art openings, exhibitions, and studio visits.

To my delight, the Chinese have no difficulty understanding that I—who look just like them—am American. When I travel elsewhere in the world—Egypt, Italy—people sometimes have a hard time grasping this concept.

When we went out together, the students had an endearing way of offering to carry my things—coats, bags. Since Beijing is extremely dry, they were attentive in offering me tea and bottled water. But the incident that completely disarmed me happened at a class party I hosted in my apartment that devolved into the playing of games, games that were like rowdy versions of "Simon Says."

At semester's end, the students organized a potluck dinner in the graduate painting studio. When I arrived, one of the students handed me a bag of gifts—an ingenious eyebrow pencil and shaping knife, which she promptly proceeded to demonstrate on me and on her classmates. (The shaping knife was used to eliminate stray or excess eyebrow hairs. The eyebrow pencil, with its three component parts, was used to delineate a contour line around the eyebrow and fill in color to get consistent coverage, and as a final touch, had a small bristle brush for separating and combing the eyebrow hairs in upward strokes.) Some days earlier, I had complimented the student on her eyebrows—Chinese women are particularly attentive to their eyebrows, which are traditionally seen as a focal point of beauty. After dinner, we settled down to playing round after round of the parlor game "Cops and Assassins."

Compared to the master of fine art (MFA) students at the State University of New York at New Paltz, where I have taught for two decades, the Renmin graduate students seemed—not young in the sense of being immature—but somewhat naïve. They *are* younger—most of them enter the graduate program directly out of college, whereas the majority of our MFA students have had some life experience. Returning to school, the American students know that spending two years immersed in a full-time graduate art program is a privilege; most of them pay for their own education, often with student loans. They also clearly understand that once they graduate, in spite of having an MFA degree, like most artists, they will have to take up a day job; whereas my Renmin graduate students seemed to entertain vague ideas about life after school, a condition I associate more with undergraduate students. In China, students who attend public universities like Renmin pay minimal tuition; they cover their own living expenses, but those costs are also modest.[1]

I was keenly aware of my lack of knowledge and understanding of how Chinese society functioned. In the US, although it is helpful to have connections, you do not *have* to be connected to get a job. In China, I noticed that a lot of my own Chinese cousins' children had "inherited" jobs from their fathers. That is, if their college studies related to their fathers', they would gain entry into the firm—especially if the jobs were governmental (in schools, hospitals, or city government); a couple of my cousins literally vacated their positions to their offspring by retiring.

From what I could tell, none of my students came from artistic backgrounds; they were clearly striking out on their own. A couple of them were or had been primary school art teachers, and the master's degree would qualify them for high-school teaching. In the US, the MFA is a terminal degree. It qualifies you to teach at the university level. Currently in China, you need to have a PhD to teach at a university, although it is not uncommon to be hired with a master's degree and be given a period of time to complete a PhD.

Life in China for the Chinese is complicated by the *Hukou*, a kind of passport system that restricts access to government-funded services (like education and health care) to the birthplace of the holder. A Chinese citizen cannot relocate at will. A provincial student gets access to residence in Beijing if he or she is accepted into a Beijing university; otherwise, a person can only legitimately move to another city if he or she gains employment in that city. Residency in Beijing is highly prized because the city offers more employment opportunities and because it is urban and culturally sophisticated.

I asked some of the students why they chose to attend Renmin University and was surprised when all but one of them said they had come because of their professor. (They met the professor at the university in their home province; when the professor joined the Renmin faculty, they followed to Beijing.) I asked Yaning, the student who entered Renmin without a professorial connection, if knowing a professor increased the likelihood of getting accepted to the college, and she replied with an emphatic "Yes!" Renmin University is prestigious, and entry is highly competitive: it took her two tries to get accepted. She also said that in China you cannot enter a PhD program unless a professor agrees beforehand to be your advisor, and professors only take on two advisees a year.

Professor Guo Chunning, a Renmin art department colleague, said that a close connection to a professor benefits a student because university professors can be well connected, and in China, many art positions and opportunities are governmentally funded. Lest I sound judgmental or sanctimonious, let me admit that there was a time not so long ago in the US that art department teaching jobs were handed out in similar ways. For decades, if you graduated with an MFA from Yale, you were almost guaranteed a college teaching job, and the alums laughingly referred to "the Yale Mafia" for the number of prestigious art prizes, like the Tiffany or the Rome Academy fellowship, won by the MFA alums. When I was hired into the SUNY New Paltz Art Department in 1997, one of the older art professors off-handedly asked, "Who does she know?"

II

The larger cultural gap I encountered in China involved teaching. I developed a deep attachment to my students, but I came away confused by what I considered to be strange gaps in their education—by their inability to do certain basic tasks or perceive and articulate some elemental visual aspects of two-dimensional composition. My class at Renmin University was made up of graduate students majoring in "Western" painting as well as "Chinese" painting—in China, they are seen as separate disciplines.

For an artist like me, who has spent most of her painting career working with a visual vocabulary inspired by Middle Eastern and Far Eastern art, it was with interest that I came to realize while in China that my students did not know what to make of my layered, highly patterned mandala-like paintings. My most advanced graduate student, Hong Xing, admitted to me that he found my work to be (only) decorative.

One of the lectures I gave when I traveled across China was titled *Double Vision: Reconciling my Eastern Visual Sensibility with a Western Art Education*. In the lecture, I posited that Western art tradition, which descends from Ancient Classical Greek and Roman art, privileges man, or at least the human figure, as centrally important. This viewpoint differs distinctly from Middle Eastern and Far Eastern art traditions, which do not fetishize the human form—except in the guise of the Buddha or the Gods.

In a Chinese ink painting, a figure, a house, or a bridge is gently inserted into the landscape, occupying no more, and usually less, visual importance than a tree, a hill, or a body of water. The same applies to built pavilions, pagodas, and bridges that are designed to blend in with, not dominate, the landscape. Contrast this with the imposing roads, bridges, aqueducts, temples, and amphitheaters the Ancient Romans constructed across Western Europe.

Chinese landscape painting, also known as scholar painting, was historically a refined and elitist art form practiced by noblemen and the literati. It was never an art of the people. The popular or commonplace art—porcelain wares, tiles, bronze vessels, cloisonné, or fabric design—in China, Japan, India, and the Middle East tended to be bright, colorful, patterned, and ornamented. What underlies public or popular Middle and Far Eastern art is a more decentralized, dispersed conception of the world that is consistently and insistently conveyed through the use of repetitive patterns. Visually, this kind of repetition flattens hierarchy: what you sense is a pervasive, consistent, almost hypnotic evenness. No one component is more important than another, including man. And it is from this more popular and utilitarian art that I draw inspiration for my work.

European art with its dominant Classicism has not marched forward uninterruptedly in the West. There have been, in fact, two distinct periods when it fell out of fashion. The first occurred in the Middle Ages, starting with the Holy Roman Empire, when the flatness of Byzantine art overtook the Classical; in fact, for hundreds of years, the technique of Classical rendering was forgotten and essentially lost until it was revived in the Italian Renaissance. The second period of time when traditional Classicism was set aside in the West happened in the first half of the twentieth century with the advent of movements such as Cubism, Surrealism, Abstraction, Dada, Abstract Expressionism, Minimalism, Land Art, and Color Field Painting.

It is this second period that is relevant to this discussion. I will show how China's adoption of Western painting was indelibly affected by a twist of historical fate that prevented the Chinese from undergoing and experiencing Modernism as it unfolded in the twentieth century.

III

Like Russia, China in the 1910s experienced staggering political change. The Qing Dynasty was overthrown in 1912; revolution was in the air, and "reform-minded Chinese debated how to modernize their nation."[2] Chinese scholars left to study abroad; in the 1920s and '30s, Paris received two waves of Chinese student-artists. (A number of Chinese artists were accepted into the Académie des Beaux-Arts, and a large survey of work by Chinese artists in Paris was commemorated by an exhibition at the Jeu de Paume.)[3] Although some of these artists remained in Paris, the majority returned to China, bringing with them the new medium of oil painting. In 1949, after the Japanese were expulsed and the Kuomintang government routed to Taiwan, the Communist Party took control of China. For the next thirty years, until the death of Mao Zedong in 1976, China would be closed to the West.

By 1949–1950, the USSR had become China's closest ally. In the summer of 1949, a delegation of Chinese Communist Party leaders traveled to Russia to confer with Stalin and the Soviet leadership. The delegation stayed for three months and made a series of requests of the USSR for financial and educational aid. In a July 6, 1949, letter to Stalin, the Chinese asked to be allowed to study Russia's public administration, requested Russia's help in developing postal, telegraphic, and air service between the two nations, asked Russia to train the Chinese Navy and Air Force (including the building and repairing of aircrafts), and expressed the desire to establish a closer cultural relationship with the Soviet Union.[4]

Today, just as there are scattered remnants of Soviet-built industrial structures across China—such as the East German factories now occupied by art galleries in Beijing's 798 Art District—there remains in China, less visible but possibly more deeply embedded, systems acquired from the Soviets, and the Chinese system of art education is one of them.

IV

Currently in China, children who are interested in art are taught to render realistically from life. The Chinese have adopted wholesale the tradition of Western art as it was inherited from Ancient Classical Greeks and Romans, and their understanding of space is grounded on the Italian Renaissance discoveries of one- and two-point perspective.

Prior to my semester in Beijing, I had encountered only one student from Mainland China. Mei had completed a master of art in painting at another

American university prior to entering our MFA program. Despite that experience, she stubbornly held to certain notions about contemporary painting that conflicted with our understanding on the subject. In the current art world, anything goes: work can be figurative, abstract, illustrative, political, material, conceptual, narrative, appropriated. There is no one dominating movement or medium; all approaches and media are seen as equally valid.

It was disconcerting to have Mei insist that she wanted to make "modern art" because that turned out to be a series of acrylic wash paintings on large sheets of paper with a loose, clumsily painted female figure immersed in water. She seemed to believe that rendering the figures badly was precisely what made her work "modern" and expressive, which struck me as a superficial and simplistic, not to say misguided, approach to abstraction.

I had a similar experience at Renmin University, where I met an oil painting graduate student, Yu Chun, who had a gift for figurative work. He wasn't just good at rendering figures; he had the ability to make his figures unusually expressive, yet he insisted that he did not want to paint representationally. He wanted to make abstract paintings. He showed me painting after abstract painting he had started and abandoned. Clearly, he was having difficulty moving forward.

Encouraged by Fulbright, I crisscrossed China, lecturing at universities and art academies, getting glimpses into a wide variety of art departments, among them three of the six Chinese art academies, all impressively large, newly constructed campuses where an entire multi-story building housed a single discipline, like sculpture—quite a contrast to a vocational college in Hangzhou that offered a much shallower art education, where teaching a discipline such as ceramics is crammed into six short weeks of study. One of the more interesting places I visited was Xinjiang University in Urumqi, capital of the Uyghur Autonomous Region, where the art department only offered two disciplines, graphic design and fashion design. My hosts were two professors, Ablat Boshi, an ethnic Uighur, and An Xiaobo, an ethnic Manchurian.

Professor Ablat and his wife had traveled to the US, where they toured art museums. Back home, he wanted to make abstract paintings. (He did his graduate studies in the former Soviet Union; prior to this, he had painted portraits and landscapes.) He said, "Representational painting is of the past; abstraction is today." Looking at his paintings, I could see that he, too, was hitting a roadblock with his work.

I am sympathetic to these painters – not because abstraction is more current than representation but because being able to perceive and understand abstract visual language is essential to understanding contemporary visual art. A prime characteristic that runs through most modern and contemporary art is that the work is undergirded by abstract qualities encapsulated by what we call Formalism. Formalism is based on the relationship between the abstract elements of art, which consist of color, value, line, form, shape, space, texture, and pattern.[5]

The main difficulty for realist artists moving into abstraction lies in the need to negotiate a different sense of space. An artist who has only learned to paint representationally can perceive perspectival space, overlapping space, and stacked Chinese painting space, but she does not know how to see in terms of abstract space.

Of course, every artist works with the elements of art, but when you work abstractly, that is, when you take away the "thingness" of the subject, you automatically change the nature of the space in the painting. Without "things" (like a person, a stand of trees, a bowl of fruit), there is no need for a "realistic" sense of space; the laws of gravity need not apply, nor do we insist on having a unified sense of light. The paradigm shift is so extreme that unless the artist has been taught how to see abstract relationships, she will be lost; the traditional bearings she has always relied on are missing.

This was the condition of my former student Mei and the two painters I met in China. I knew they were failing to understand something, but I did not know what it was. Only after returning home, where I sought out Mei, exchanged texts with Professor An Xiaobo of Xinjiang University, and queried Maxine Leu, a New Paltz graduate student from Taiwan, did I finally dig down to the root of the problem.

In one form or another, college-level art education in the industrialized countries teaches the design principles on which Modernism is based. The Bauhaus School in Germany codified these design principles and established a *Vorkurs* (preliminary course) that taught students how to work with color, value, line, form, shape, space, texture, and pattern isolated from representation.[6] Also known as the International Style, Modernist aesthetics cut a broad swath across the globe in architecture, graphic design, and much of industrial design and fine art. Because the Bauhaus was a school as well as an art movement, the faculty and students who fled Germany before and during the outbreak of World War II taught Bauhaus-based education methods wherever they landed—in Europe and the Americas—but China and the Soviet Republics, cocooned in their self-imposed silos, were cut off from this larger artistic conversation taking place in the world.

Today, contemporary Chinese artists and art students are familiar with the history of Western art, including Modernism. Simply teaching Bauhaus design principles as theory in lecture classes, as it is currently done in China, does not work. Most art forms, like athletics, belong to a category of cognition known as embodied knowledge. Embodied learning is acquired only when the body and its senses are engaged, not just the brain. You cannot teach a person to sing by lecturing to him or her about singing; people learn to sing by singing. Learning to see color relationships, seeing the compositional interaction between positive and negative shapes, or understanding the spatial effects of color—must all be experienced visually and the knowledge acquired physically, through trial and error.

Chinese artists who have not had the benefit of a Bauhaus-based studio education acquired their knowledge of Bauhaus principles only through book learning, so to speak; because they were not physically trained to work with the visual phenomena, they have not been sensitized, and as a consequence, they either do not see or do not look for their effects. Basically, the art schools in China do not realize the importance of training students to use these principles in studio courses, and the faculty, because they themselves have not been trained, do not know how to teach it.

A consistent and notable thing I found with art students in China was how little they regarded space. Even students who were clearly working with a sense of landscape were at times unable to describe the space in their work. In China, working with the students, I kept coming up against what I can only describe as an astonishing level of space-related visual illiteracy. It was as if, in their art education, space was never discussed.

When I returned home and met up with my former student, Mei, I pointedly asked what she saw when she looked at the work of her MFA classmate, Brooke Long, who made architecturally inflected abstract paintings.

Mei said, "I see color, shapes, lines, and rhythm."

I asked, "What about space?"

She looked at me, tilted her head, repeated, "Space?" and blankly shook her head.

A year later in 2018, I returned to China and met with my former students at Renmin University. By then, I had completed a draft of this chapter and could tell them of my findings. The penny dropped when Yu Chun, the student who tried, unsuccessfully, to paint abstractly, admitted that he only considers the lateral space in his artwork, not the depth!

The two incidents confirmed what I had experienced in China. The students—whether they painted representationally or abstractly—were literally not looking at, much less giving consideration to, spatial depth in their paintings.

Ironically, it is in painting—a two-dimensional art form—that space is most present, most manipulated, most dramatic. Sculptures have bulk and sit in space, as does installation art, but they do not manipulate the space around themselves. Painting, in contrast, using the magic of illusion, can flatten space, exaggerate perspective, deepen space, contort space, invent space, and spatially fool the eye. Most people, when asked, would probably say that color is what makes painting and drawing unique mediums, but sculptures, photographs, and installations can also employ color; it is the possibilities of creating and inventing space that make painting and drawing singular.

VI

It should also be noted that the Soviets did not aim to produce fine artists; they were training art workers. Art workers are distinguished not by a personal vision as much as by accomplished skill and craft. To produce an art worker, you emphasize skill training, and Chinese art students are generally quite skilled. A sculptural course on the figure at a Chinese art academy might begin with students copying Roman busts and Renaissance sculptures before they go on to copy a wide range of ancient styles of Chinese Buddhist and dynastic sculptures. Chinese professors are conscientious about passing down traditions of fabrication. Skilled graduates from such programs of study are able to restore, repair, and imitate ancient artwork. To acquire this level of skill is arduous and time consuming; it swallows up the majority of the time and energy of a student undergoing four years of college.

In comparison, US art education is usually less insistent on teaching skills. Skills are taught, of course, but at least as much emphasis is placed on helping the art student develop her individual voice, her subject matter and concepts. Without development in these areas, it is hard for an artist to become self-actualized, and she is likely to remain a "mere" craftsperson.

This brings me to the most startling discovery I made while in China. It occurred around midterm when I scheduled a class critique. Arriving at the student's studio, I was surprised and mildly annoyed to see she had not set up her artwork. I asked her to do so and was irritated by the haphazard way she proceeded. (Artworks are seen in context, and it is important how work is presented.) I moved things around, and when the work was passably set up, I turned to the class and asked them to start the crit. They looked at me in confusion and then at each other, which caused me to look back at them with equal lack of comprehension. It took a couple of beats before I caught on—the students did not know how to start because they had never held a class critique before!

Coming out of an American system of art education, I was unable to conceive of this. In American pedagogy, the class critique is how students are trained to "see." Critiques discipline students to speak analytically about artwork because they are forced to articulate what they see and how they see. When the artwork of a particular student is being discussed, she receives feedback that allows her to hear how her work is being received, read, understood, interpreted, or misinterpreted.

In his art blog, Kurt Ralske explains the centrality of the group crit in American art schools:

The Crit

The word "crit" is not found in the dictionary, and is not used in normal conversation. But to those in art school, it's a term that points to the center of the universe. Here, "crit" means the most essential and familiar of events: the critique session, in which a student's artwork is formally evaluated by a group of faculty and students. A student presents his work, and the group responds with feedback: comments, questions, advice, cheers, jeers, and tears.[7]

The flip side of not integrating class crits into studio art courses is that the professor, by default, becomes the single "authority" in the classroom since she does all the talking. The students are not given a structured forum that demands their verbal participation, their active engagement. This top-down aspect of art education reflects the top-down structure of the Chinese and Soviet governments.

The regrettable result of not being trained to speak in class crits is that students are left unable to verbally analyze what they see. This was demonstrated to me at the end of the semester: I took some students to the Faurschou Foundation to see a small retrospective of paintings by the Scottish painter Peter Doig, which included Doig's early paintings—the landscapes he made during and immediately after graduate school.

When we walked into the gallery, we immediately felt uplifted by the paintings; the students and I caught each other's eyes, nodded, and smiled.

As I stood in the first room surveying the paintings, my student Hong Xing asked me, "Are you able to say why a painting is good?"

I said, "Yes, I can. Why? Can't you?"

He said, "No, not really."

So I gathered the students in front of the first painting and "modeled" for them how I looked at the painting. I said, "These are landscape paintings, but they are not like any landscapes you have ever seen before, right? That the artist managed to do this is already remarkable. Landscapes have a very long tradition; it isn't easy to bring something new to a landscape." I then did a formal analysis of the painting, talking about the visual effects Doig achieved and how he achieved them—the range of paint application, the layers of information the painting delivered, the variety and inventiveness of his visual vocabulary, and the spatial complexity of the painting. I then took them around the gallery doing the same with a few of the other paintings in the show.

That this occurred at the end of the semester was unfortunate and frustrating. I had been with these students for three months, but because their art training had been so different from my own, I was slow on the uptake. I had to hear, see, or experience a student's inability to do something before I could perceive the deficit. This made me feel foolish and negligent as a teacher. But it wasn't negligence; it was a failure of imagination on my part. Apparently, I was so conditioned by the style and sequencing of American art education that I could not imagine a system that left out such important and fundamental art-teaching practices.

Notes

1. Jason Lim, "Why China Doesn't Have a Student Debt Problem," *Forbes*, August 29, 2016. Web. 30 September 2019.
2. "Pioneers of Modern Chinese Painting in Paris: Chu Teh-Chun, Lin Fengmian, SanYu, T'ang Hatwen, Wu Dayu, Wu Guangzhong, Xu Beihong, Siong Bingming, Zao Wou-ki," *deSarthe.com*, May 12, 2014. Web. 18 April 2018.
3. Fionnuala McHugh, "Exhibition Illuminates Chinese Artists Who Lived in Paris in the 20th Century," *South China Morning Post*, International Edition, November 1, 2017. Web. 26 April 2018.
4. Dieter Heinzig, *The Soviet Union and Communist China 1945–1950: The Arduous Road to the Alliance* (Armonk, NY: ME Sharpe, 2004). Print.
5. Simon Morley, "In Praise of Vagueness: Re-Visioning the Relationship between Theory and Practice in the Teaching of Fine Art from a Cross-Cultural Perspective," *Journal of Visual Practice* 16, no. 2 (February 23, 2017): 87–103. Web. 30 April 2018.
6. Ibid.
7. Kurt Ralske, "The Crit," *Kurt Ralske (blog)*, May 2011. Web. 26 April 2018.

7 Teaching American Government in the People's Republic of China

Jeannette W. Cockroft

I have been in love with China my entire life. As a New England teenager in the 1970s, I read Mao's *Little Red Book* and wanted to join the revolution. I studied Chinese language and culture as an undergraduate and later, pursued a PhD in history in which one of my areas of study was modern Chinese social history. Upon graduation, I taught English at Suzhou University in Jiangsu province. I later spent a summer teaching English at an immersive language camp outside Hangzhou.

The challenge of conducting daily life in Mandarin and exploring the juxtaposition of an ancient culture with the twenty-first century turned the most mundane tasks into adventures. The sense of accomplishment was exhilarating. And when the results of my adventures were awkward or embarrassing, Chinese friends and colleagues were patient and accommodating. Returning to my full-time job in the United States was always bittersweet; I missed the challenges of living in China. After fourteen years of full-time teaching, I applied for a Fulbright lecturer opportunity in China and was thrilled to be chosen.

I spent the 2016–2017 academic year in the College of Political Science and Public Administration at Southwest University in Chongqing, southwest China, teaching introductory American government to freshman and sophomore political science majors. The dean of the Political Science program requested two things of me. The first was to teach my students to think critically; the second was to help them improve their English language skills. Exploring the tenets of American government with unprepared and disinterested students has been routine in my teaching career. Exploring that material with students unfamiliar with the Western traditions of representative government and individualism would be a challenge. For both the students and me, that challenge would be complicated by the fact that English was the language of instruction and not all students would be equally proficient. While students were struggling to express themselves in English, I would be struggling in Mandarin to clarify my questions and instructions. An example of the synergy these struggles created is the final course exam.

On July 4, 2017, I administered the last of my final exams in the Introduction to Politics: American Government course. I had taught two sections of this course in both the fall 2016 and the spring 2017 terms. All four classes received the same exam, which was distributed before the exam period to give students time to craft their responses. There were three questions. The first asked students to identify five elements of American political culture that encouraged democracy. The second required a discussion of five elements that seemed anti-democratic. The final question directed students to write about at least one thing we had studied or that they had read about that seemed odd or inconsistent with their stereotypes of the United States.

For the first question, most students identified things that my American students would agree contribute to the creation of a democratic framework. They noted civil rights, the ownership of private property, and feminism and the rise of the women's movements. They were impressed with the many opportunities to vote and the historical efforts to extend the franchise. Others wrote about the foundational elements of democracy in uniquely Chinese or Marxist ways. Several students noted that, unlike China, the United States had never experienced a feudal period. In Marxist thought, feudalism is a historical stage of economic development in which the masses of people, or serfs, are tied to the land and must remit a portion of their production to their feudal lord. Additional students noted the anti-imperialistic nature of the American Revolution as fundamental to the creation of American democracy. Although the revolution can be described as an anti-imperialistic struggle, the perspective is simplistic in that it does not consider the myriad ways in which British political thought and experience shaped the Revolutionary period. Neither of these perspectives is inaccurate, but they do represent an ideological framework that most of my American colleagues and I define as inadequate to the task of exploring the democratic roots of the republic. We do not think about American history in these terms.

The second exam question asked students to discuss elements of American political life that might be undemocratic. Once again, students focused on structures that my American students would also identify as undemocratic. These included the failure of the Constitution to address the issue of slavery, problems of low voter turnout, and the growing concentration of executive power in the twentieth century. More interestingly, some were ambivalent regarding facets of American politics about which my American students are now also skeptical. They worried that too much free speech could legitimize divisive conspiracy theories. Unfettered free speech could facilitate the dissemination of radical Islamic propaganda. Still others believed that excessive free speech could create a tyranny of the majority, in which only officially sanctioned opinions could be expressed and less popular ones denied. They also posited that an unconstrained media report-ing a barrage of negative stories might alienate citizens. These concerns reflect a traditional Chinese preference for social harmony as well as the current government's desire for political stability. They also underscore the degree to which both Chinese and American students misunderstand the notion of a marketplace of ideas in which the most useful ideas emerge from the chaos of contention and debate.

The final question on the exam required students to analyze something in American culture that seemed strange or odd. This question was the tough-est on the exam because we had not explicitly discussed it during the term. It required students to consider their own ideas of good government; it also invited implicit comparisons to Chinese governance. Many answers were not surprising. Students thought it odd that a person without years of politi-cal experience and deep roots within a political party could parachute into the nation's top political office. For others, the idea of term limits as a way of limiting power seemed punitive to both the president and society at large. Shouldn't someone who had developed the relationships and expertise to govern effectively be allowed to serve until retirement?

The one thing that almost all students throughout the year found disturb-ing was the American gun culture. Students asked if the fear of being a victim of gun violence explained why Americans entertained in their homes rather than in public areas, such as restaurants, as the Chinese do. Others asked if the prevalence of guns indicated an abdication of the government's responsibility to provide for basic security. Did Americans perceive gun ownership as indicative of such failure? If so, then, of course, everyone needed a gun for protection. But if not, why were guns necessary? But per-haps the most poignant and pervasive question was: will I be safe if I go to study in the United States? Most were obsessed with American college life and hoped to study in the US. They shared a set of stereotypes that depicted college life as a 1950s beach movie: beautiful people engaged in nonstop laughing, singing, and dancing. These young people heard no reminders of parental sacrifice, no exhortations to work hard, and no admonition to think about their futures. They just had fun.

My students asked endless questions about college life. What sort of music and movies did my students enjoy? What was dating like? They also wondered how American students paid for college and how they themselves would be able to afford to study in the US. Some refused to believe that many of my students studied very hard, worked full-time jobs, and had no time to party.

They relished the fantasy of a frivolous, carefree student life. As South-west University undergraduates, their days started at 6:00 a.m. and often did not end until midnight. Some semesters, they spent as much as thirty hours a week in class. Some classes met on weekends to accommodate a minor as well as a major course of study. Much of the classwork required rote memorization of material presented in texts or in PowerPoint presentations. They were also expected to participate in a variety of mandatory political and social activities that left them exhausted.

Having taught in China before, I knew my students would be over-scheduled, so I structured my class in ways to make it engaging but not onerous. Using the same introductory text I had used in the US, I limited the amount of reading and created a study guide that identified key vocabulary as well as six to ten questions highlighting the main points of each chapter. Also included were a couple of short answer questions for students to practice their composition skills.

In class, we reviewed the pronunciation and meaning of each vocabulary item. I divided the class into groups and assigned one question to each group. Within each group, students worked together to answer the question and then designated a spokesperson to share that answer with the class. In the last thirty minutes of the weekly, eighty-minute class, students wrote on one of the short essays and shared their answers with the class.

This approach capitalized on the traditional Chinese preference for a collaborative search for knowledge. However, the pitfalls of doing group work with Chinese students mirrored the pitfalls of doing group work with students at my home university. Less motivated students played on their phones in the guise of doing research. Others gossiped quietly with classmates. As they thumbed through the text and then read aloud the answer to the questions, I knew many of them had not read the assignment.

Although all the students were political science majors, they were not all equally happy about it. A student's choice of university and course of study are a function of the score earned on the college entrance exam, or *gao kao*. Some were excited about being at Southwest University because of its illustrious history and reputation. Others were far from home and lonely. Some were happy to be political science majors and looked forward to becoming the government bureaucrats for which the major prepared them. Still others were confounded at ending up in a course on American government and were nervous about their first interactions with a native English speaker. Whatever their feelings about the class, they were always polite and patient.

After a few weeks, the activities intended to foster critical thinking and student engagement had become painfully routinized. Students shuffled into class and complied with my instructions but seemed disengaged. To ask students if they were bored was useless. Such an admission would be considered rude. Because I assumed that, like me, they found the predictability wearisome, I varied the order of class activities and changed the method used for choosing group members. The mood of the class did not change, and the adjustments seemed inadequate. To enliven the class and to foster more analytical engagement with the material, I devised projects that would encourage students to use the course material in more creative ways. The first required students to write a constitution for a country of their own creation. The second, later in the term, called for those same groups to create a pair of political parties for the country they had designed.

The first six chapters of our American government text dealt with the historical and intellectual foundations of the American republic. Topics included debates between Federalists and anti-Federalists on the power of the national government and the protections of citizens embodied in ideas of civil rights and civil liberties. Divided into groups of four to five, students were tasked with writing a constitution for an imaginary country. First, they had to decide what sort of country they wanted: democratic, monarchical, utopian, or something else. Then they needed to determine the powers of the national government and the number of branches it would have as well as the division of powers between the national government and its subordinate units. Finally, they defined the rights and responsibilities of citizens.

Although all students had smartphones, I had seen very few of them with laptop computers or tablets. Thus, I provided paper and markers for students to create posters that illustrated the governmental structures of the country they had created. Each group presented their work to the class and explained what they had created and why they had made the choices they made. Photos were taken for later reference.

Later in the term, after we had studied political parties, political participation, and the role of the media in the United States, a second project required students to design a pair of political parties for the country they had created earlier. This exercise was a bit more challenging because it required students to think about a civic society functioning separately from the central government. Quite likely, these students did not yet have enough background in political science to understand the varieties of civil society beyond China. But, as a natural outgrowth of class discussion, the project seemed a worthwhile endeavor. As they wrestled with the concepts of political parties, political participation, the media, and its relationship to central government, several questions were to be addressed. These included the following: What values does each party represent? What will political participation look like, and how will it be defined? What will be the role of the media? How will the parties use the media to shape public opinion? Students worked in their original groups to create a poster presentation of their work. Once again, they presented their work to the class.

The resulting projects were more imaginative than I had anticipated. A group of self-described feminists wrote a constitution in which an empress had all government power and one of the branches of government was a male consort assigned to satisfy the empress's every whim. Another group designed a democracy with three branches of government—much like the United States—in which all citizens were required to do compulsory military service in exchange for free medical attention and educational opportunities. Yet another devised a utopian country with no military because everyone was a pacifist. This government used the media to educate its citizenry on nonviolent strategies to resolve conflict. Others created a democratic authoritarian government in which citizens chose leaders who then exercised unlimited power. Its one political party represented university students and expected the media to champion the message that students should be free to make their own life choices.

At the end of each term, some students thanked me for the opportunity to explore their creativity and to make their own intellectual connections with the material. A few others, based on the little effort put forth in creating their projects, had not embraced the experience. I was intermittently frustrated that the results were not as analytical or as internally consistent between the first and second projects as I had hoped. I wondered if students were learning anything at all about American government. Ultimately, I recognized that my expectations had been unrealistic. The students had studied American government, explored innovative uses of basic concepts, and survived their first English-only political science class. They had not expected to do any of these things on the first day of the semester. In their position, I would not have handled that much uncertainty any differently. We had stretched beyond our comfort zones while getting to know each other. Those accomplishments were the crux of a successful term.

In addition to class time with students, I also established an English corner for each of my classes. When large numbers of foreigners were first allowed into China in the 1980s, young Chinese often approached tourists in public spaces, like street corners, and asked to speak English with them. The term now refers to any informal opportunity for conversational English practice. I wanted to give students the opportunity to improve their conversational English skills without the pressure of grades and with the freedom to ask whatever questions they wished.

These English corners were sparsely attended. Students already had very long days of classes, meetings, and study; they jealously guarded what little free time they had. And, as my Chinese friends pointed out, undergraduates do not always recognize a rare opportunity when they see it. I tried not to fret about numbers and focused instead on those who did participate. Over time, students would bring their friends from other schools within the university and what evolved were small groups bound together by curiosity and friendship.

At first, students asked polite, perfunctory questions. They wanted to know how long I had been in China, if this was my first trip to China, and if I liked living in Chongqing. I told them I had been to China several times and that I loved living in Chongqing. Once life in Chongqing became the topic, everyone wanted to know if I liked hot pot, a staple of the local cuisine that consists of a communal pot of spicy, boiling oil in which all sorts of meats, fish, entrails, and vegetables were cooked. Students laughed when I told them that I disliked hot pot because it made my lips numb.

As we got to know one another, the questions became more substantive. One evening, a graduate student studying American literature asked me to explain the history of Christianity. She was puzzled by the Puritan migration to the New World. She thought that familiarity with the history of Christianity would facilitate an understanding not only of the Puritan experience but also of contemporary America. Her professors had discussed the socio-economic changes shaping seventeenth-century England and the rise of European imperialism but dismissed the significance of Christianity. I fumbled around the front of the classroom until I found a piece of chalk and then began a timeline on the blackboard. I started with Jesus Christ and then moved on to the establishment of the Roman Catholic Church and eventually to the Renaissance and Reformation. After about ten minutes, I asked if she understood. She nodded and thanked me. I am not sure how much she had really understood, but she had copied the timeline, which now covered nearly the entire board, for future reference.

Religion is a complex subject in China. The central government encourages traditional Chinese spiritual practices, such as Daoism and Confucianism, to constrain rampant greed and corruption. Yet, religious traditions defined as non-Chinese are highly suspect. The monotheistic faiths of Islam and Christianity challenge the power of the state by proclaiming that all people have God-given rights that cannot be superseded by government. Although the current constitution of the People's Republic of China protects the right of individuals to believe or not to believe, it also grants the government the power to limit religious practices it defines as disruptive to social harmony or injurious to the health of society.[1] Muslims in the western province of Xinjiang are monitored as a possible terrorist threat. Buddhists in Tibet who oppose Han Chinese rule are viewed as possible separatists. Among Christian denominations are the officially organized Three-Self Protestant Church, the China Christian Council, and the Patriotic Catholic Church, as a well as a myriad of unsanctioned house churches and underground churches. The line separating religious freedom from disruptive behavior often seemed arbitrary, and as a result, I was reluctant to discuss religion. As a foreign scholar, I would probably suffer nothing more severe than expulsion from China for being a disruptive influence. Disruptive students might face serious unanticipated and lifelong consequences. Yet, students often asked me about my religious life.

One of the students in English corner during the spring 2017 term was a graduate student in logic. As I got to know him, he asked me about my faith: What did I think about the Bible? Did I like Christianity? These were odd questions, and I did not understand what he was asking. While on a group sightseeing trip around Chongqing, he again asked me about the Bible. He noted that he could not always understand his bilingual version. To him, the language seemed stilted and perhaps even inaccurate. He wanted to know where he could buy an English translation of the Bible. A girl in our group suggested Taobao.com, one of the largest e-commerce sites in the country, if not in the world.[2]

I did not understand why he dismissed her suggestion. I have a translated copy of the New Testament purchased about fifteen years ago in a Suzhou foreign language bookstore. Perhaps he did not want anyone to know that he had bought one. Perhaps he had financial issues. Ultimately, the reason is unimportant. After a few moments' consideration, I offered him my copy.

Giving up a Bible that I had owned for more than thirty years was difficult. But I chose to embody the message of generosity exemplified by the book that I could easily replace. As the students and I approached the foreign faculty housing in which I lived, I invited him to my apartment. He quietly stood by the front door as I retrieved the Bible from the bedroom nightstand and handed it to him. He thanked me and left. After that evening, every time I saw him on campus, that Bible was tucked under his arm.

Religion was not the only serious topic about which students were curious. Young women throughout the year asked if I were a feminist. I always replied that I was. Unlike most of my American students, young Chinese women were very interested in American feminism. One day after class, a student auditing my class offered to take me sightseeing around Chongqing with a group of her friends. I loved spending time with students, so I agreed.

This student, an earnest young woman named Hui Zhi, had earlier explained the odd reaction my name had garnered throughout the academic year. Given the tonal and rhythmic differences between English and Chinese, Chinese learners of English often adopt an English name and Chinese students, an English one. Although I have a Chinese name, I decided for the sake of simplicity that my friends and students should just call me "JJ." On my first day of class in the fall term, students laughed as soon as I wrote "JJ" on the board. Someone in the class explained that it was the Chinese name of the main character in the cartoon series *Adventures of Tintin*.

The next term, when I put my name on the board and students giggled, I acknowledged that I realized that it was a reference to *Tintin*. The snickering grew louder and continued for several minutes. As I began to delineate my expectations for the term, the students settled down and the class moved on. However, after all the other students had left at the end of the class, Hui

Zhi explained that "JJ" was local slang for penis. As I nodded, she kept repeating, "It's a man's dick." I kept nodding, and she kept repeating. In that moment, I did not know which I wanted more: for her to stop talking or for the building to collapse onto me and end my embarrassment. After a few more repetitions, she seemed satisfied that I had understood, so she stopped talking and left the room.

When the Saturday came for Hui Zhi, her friends, and I to sightsee, we had a wonderful day. Walking around the Yuzhong part of the city, we visited St. Joseph's Catholic cathedral and saw the Tonguanmin City Wall, dating back to the early Ming period. At midafternoon, we had coffee and snacks at a cozy, Western-style house converted into a café and hostel. At this point, I realized the purpose of the invitation. They wanted to talk about feminism.

They all identified as lesbians and wanted to know if my being single was a feminist statement. I replied that, as a product of the women's movement in the 1970s, I had been a feminist my entire life but was not a lesbian. I added that I had been married but was now happily single and childless. The idea that a middle-aged woman could choose to be both single and childless puzzled them. But the possibility of a married feminist was incomprehensible. Their questions were reminiscent of the extremist views of the women's movement, which claimed that the inherently patriarchal nature of marriage and family oppressed all women. The only way for women to achieve their full potential and to live satisfying lives was to reject these social constraints and to choose a liberated life lived in the company of women only. I often wonder if these students really were lesbians. Perhaps they were simply rejecting the patriarchal expectations of marriage, childrearing, and subordinate status that continue to constrain the lives of Chinese women.

While at Southwest University, I developed relationships that facilitated the discussion of many topics. With friends, students, and colleagues, I explored subjects ranging from Donald Trump and gender in American politics to prehistorical Chinese artifacts to cat cafés and the virtues of designer lipsticks. At the same time, we all seemed to understand that some topics were off limits. Leading the list of taboo topics are the so-called "Three Ts": Tibet, Taiwan, and Tian An Men Square. Because students never asked about these issues, I assume they accepted the government's perspective on these matters as sacrosanct. Every Fulbrighter to China is explicitly admonished not to mention these. Years earlier, while teaching English at Suzhou University, I had heard the story of a foreigner teacher dismissed for telling his students that some people outside of China under some circumstances might support the independence of Taiwan. Unwilling to risk attenuating my time in China, I avoided these sensitive topics.

Self-censorship is a curious phenomenon. Over time, I easily forgot that some ideas were proscribed because so many others were not. The nightly news on the English language television channel (Chinese Global Television Network, or CGTN) teemed with political discussions. Some questioned the wisdom of infrastructure investments connected to the One Belt, One Road initiative through which China will likely become a major power. With Beijing hosting the 2022 Winter Olympics, government efforts to nurture involvement in winter sports, such as ice hockey, also garnered media attention. In Chongqing, debate often centered on the central government's goal of eliminating poverty by 2020. I met at least two faculty members developing pilot projects for poverty alleviation programs. During the 2016 presidential election, American life and politics was a persistent topic for everyone.

The social boundaries created by this self-censorship are reinforced by a pervasive, yet nearly invisible, network of cameras. Video cameras existed in every classroom and were monitored in every building by a centrally located security guard. Walking past the control room in the building where my office was located, I could see the video feed from every classroom in the building but never heard any sound. Perhaps the sound capability had been turned off, or perhaps, it was nonexistent. These cameras in conjunction with those being installed in public outdoor spaces all over China underscore the government's effort to create an extensive surveillance state. I met both Chinese and foreign faculty who, although they expressed discomfort with the growing surveillance, accepted it as a fact of daily life. Over time, I ignored the cameras within my classroom and within my community. I thought I was doing and speaking as I pleased. Such is the pernicious nature of self-censorship.

An American colleague once noted that a Fulbrighter is essentially a "professional American." The competitive selection process and academic prestige associated with the Fulbright Program do create a sense that Fulbrighters are experts on all things American. Although reluctant to criticize the United States in front of an American guest, students were curious about everything and never hesitated to ask questions. I relished the challenge of thinking on my feet, even when the questions were beyond my narrow disciplinary expertise. As a visiting faculty member, I was also a safe person with whom students could explore all sorts of perspectives and questions. In turn, students answered my questions about their lives, families, and personal struggles. Their generosity gave me a window into contemporary Chinese life I would not have had otherwise.

One of those students commented at the end of the academic year that more Chinese students should study the American political system. Because the American and Chinese political systems function so differently, he thought mutual understanding would be enhanced if Chinese citizens understood the noisy, pluralistic, and sometimes chaotic process of American decision making. Americans, in turn, would benefit from understanding how Chinese policymakers operate. During my year at Southwest University, several of my students and colleagues became close friends with whom I continue to communicate. These friendships have become the foundation for long-term collaboration both in person and through social media that will further that mutual understanding.

Notes

1. *Center on Religion and Chinese Society at Purdue University.* Web. 14 April 2018.
2. Grace Tsai, Xinyan Yu, and Mimi Lau, "China's Online Retailers Pull Bible Off Shelves as Beijing Gets Strict on Sale of Holy Text," *South China Morning Post*, International ed., April 8, 2018. Web. 14 April 2018.

8   Stoicism Unwound

Teaching About Emotional Literacy in China

Mary Ni

Prelude

Life is full of ups and downs. I was elated to receive a ten-month-long Fulbright Teaching Award to China in spring 2016. At the same time, I was challenged to see if I would actually be able to go. I had suffered an incapacitating stroke in the winter of 2015, which resulted in the paralysis of my entire left side. I was in the midst of intensive rehabilitation and physical therapy. Simultaneously, while requesting to return to work part-time, I found all courses I usually taught had been unexplainably removed from my teaching load. This did not seem like the best time to go overseas. However, how often does a Fulbright Award fall into one's lap? With permission from Fulbright to reduce my time in China from ten to five months and delaying my employment problems until I returned, I decided to claim this extraordinary opportunity. I continued to work diligently on my physical rehabilitation, passed all the requisite medical examinations, and with much excitement and a bit of trepidation, left for Changchun in February 2017.

Background

My life choices and conflicts are grounded in a history of bias and redemption endured as an American of Chinese heritage. How I am seen and how people have treated me as "other" has shaped how I have also viewed myself. Too often perceived with ambivalence in the US, my "Chineseness" has continued to draw me back to China, again and again, in my search for belonging. Despite my lack of Chinese language and literacy skills and my lack of Chinese cultural and historical knowledge, I have felt tied to China. I somehow acquired a deep desire to know and nurture people who look like me and with whom I feel I can relate, even if in a motherland that is in many ways unfamiliar but still feels, somehow, like home.

First of all, I am a full-blooded American citizen, a first-generation Chinese-American. Throughout my life, however, I have often been seen as foreign in the United States, my country of birth. My parents erased our Chinese-ness as much as possible in their well-meaning attempts to help us better assimilate into American life. Hence, my two brothers and I were not taught to speak Chinese, nor were we educated about our Chinese culture. We were "whitewashed." And it worked.

My desire to be white was unconscious and grew stealthily with time. It became so strong that I was uneasy catching glimpses of myself in a mirror when with other white people who were also reflected back to me: It was a stark reminder that I looked different from them. In rural Maryland, looking quite different from the black minority and the white majority, I easily decided if I had to choose an identity (which it seemed that I did), I chose to be white.

Yet my own Chinese-ness and my relationship to China was fueled by a life-changing event that occurred in my early twenties. At that time, I attended a day-long workshop exclusively for nonwhite people in the Re-evaluation Counseling[1] community. The primary activity in this program was to listen closely to one another without interrupting or judging and to notice and accept the expression and release of any emotions.

When the facilitator asked for a volunteer to answer the question, "What was it like to be (fill in your ethnic group) and grow up in America?" I was the first person to raise my hand. In the process of responding to this question, I had the biggest epiphany of my life. Speaking, uninterruptedly, to this friendly group of strangers, I found huge, unusual waves of sadness and anger wash over me, and I started to cry. Instead of distracting me from my tears, the group absorbed and welcomed my release. I cried and talked and told stories of rejection, pain, cruelty, and dismissal that I had never told anyone before. People's attention was rapt. And years and years of misery and pent-up emotions were discharged. After me, others also took a turn to speak. Each participant told a remarkable story of pain, endurance, and survival.

I was transformed by this experience. Treated harshly by insensitive authority figures and bullies, I realized we all had blamed ourselves for mistreatment and confusions that were not our fault. Exposed to empty lessons, misinformation, or downright lies, we had all made misguided assumptions about how the world worked. Deceived by popularly supported myths, I realized things were often not just or fair. I realized I would never be able to pass as white, for example. What forces, in the first place, I wondered, pulled me to hate my Asian face?

The Vow

In that moment, I vowed, with the rest of my life, to learn more about the inequities and the imbalanced dynamics of race, privilege, power, and difference. I wanted to fill in my gaps in knowledge and to help right what was wrong. How could I help remove the self-made and social barriers we construct around ourselves? How could I help spare others—particularly other clueless Chinese like my younger self—the pain of ignorance, misguided thinking, and self-blame? What could I do to make the world a better place—to make the world the kind of place that I would be happy and safe to live in?

Emotional pain is a universal phenomenon that transcends cultures. The trauma of persistent, chronic emotional pain constricts our lives in unpredictable and damaging ways. Alternatively, healing from this pain is freeing and life affirming, as I had learned from my own experiences with the co-counseling paradigm. It is this foundational paradigm that spoke to me and from which I based my psychological work.

I was cautioned, however, by professionals in the field that traditional Chinese people would not be open to "touchy-feely" psychological frameworks or the personal sharing of feelings. The Chinese, I was told, somaticized their emotional pain, converting painful mental states, like anxiety, for example, into headaches or stomachaches. The Chinese, experts admonished, would not be a good group to teach and practice a self-help paradigm that heavily relied on one's ability to talk about and express personal feelings. Yet, however "whitewashed" I was, despite growing up in a Chinese household where feelings were not discussed, I found this method worked for me. Consequently, I felt challenged to find out and possibly disprove these cautionary tales.

In previous trips and work in China, I had gained confidence that the peer counseling/emotional literacy[2] paradigm I had learned and practiced—despite differences in Eastern and Western cultural sensibilities—could be very effective with native Chinese people. In this most recent Fulbright teaching experience, I hoped to not only teach emotional literacy concepts over time but also see if something bigger could develop: a program or ongoing project?

Changchun

The Chinese government collaborating with the Fulbright selection committee placed me at Northeast Normal University (NENU) in the northeastern city of Changchun. Oblivious to this populous six-million-plus-person city before I arrived, I found it to be a historically rich, flourishing, enjoyable metropolis. The school itself was welcoming and full of possibilities.

Upon arriving in Changchun, I was given a one-bedroom apartment, with an adjoining kitchen, in a foreign experts building that also functioned as a hotel. Conveniently, there was a big grocery and department store around the corner from my building, as well as many shops, restaurants, street vendors, banks, parks, schools, and bustling places of business. My campus was an easy twenty-minute walk away. Rush-hour traffic was loud, impatient, and filled with honking vehicles. Negotiating the streets could be dangerous even with streetlights and pedestrian crossing signs.

Physically, I fit right in. My style of dress and my facial features allowed me to walk anonymously down any street. When walking to work on my first day, for example, a stranger stopped me to ask for directions. I smiled to myself as I told him that I was not from Changchun. Indeed, I could "pass" physically but was lacking in so many other ways: I couldn't read the street names, shop signs, or advertisements. I couldn't understand much of the spoken Chinese of the passersby.

Teaching About Emotional Literacy

> To be emotionally literate is to be able to handle emotions in a way that improves your personal power and the quality of your life and—equally important—the quality of life of the people around you. Emotional literacy helps your emotions work *for you* instead of against you. It improves relationships, creates loving possibilities between people, makes cooperative work possible, and facilitates the feeling of community.[3]

In teaching a specific course about emotional literacy in China, I invited students to join me in an experimental setting, which gave them an opportunity to learn theory and then move quickly to practice, using each other as respected experimental subjects and researchers. Early on, we developed a class contract, specifying the types of behaviors, attitudes, and responsibilities students desired of each other. I also clarified my own goals: 1) to facilitate the building of an effective, supportive classroom community; 2) to provide and discuss essential theoretical information; 3) to allow opportunities to observe and practice new skills; and 4) to make time for personal, shared self-reflection.

My formal workload was agreeably light: to teach one graduate student class in the School of Education. I was also asked to develop a series of workshops/lectures for my host university, as well as for other places[4] in China. Lecturing and demonstrating about the theory and practice of emotional literacy was the focus of my work.

Teaching only one class allowed me more time to pay attention to students, their weekly papers, and their progress. For example, students were required to participate in weekly paired sessions with a class partner in order to practice deep listening, honest speaking, and relationship building.

With my extra time, I set up one- to two-hour-long individual supervisory sessions, first with each student and later with each student pair or trio.

As a part of doing these supervisory sessions, I was also a participant in the listening and speaking time with each student to model the possibilities and value of vulnerability and to lessen the teacher/student divide. We would each take turns speaking (and listening), uninterruptedly, for a set amount of time, about our choice of subject. Then, I would process the experience with them. What was it like to speak in this session? What was it like to listen? What feelings arose and were released in yourself as listener? As speaker? Did you learn anything useful about yourself or about the process? Do you have any questions or concerns at this point? And so forth . . .

My sense of connection to each student deepened with each class and each individual meeting. I found these students (mostly native Chinese but also from Indonesia, Thailand, Uganda, and Mongolia) were remarkably open and trusting with me. As time went by, they shared very personal and sometimes emotional and painful stories from their lives. Students also shared affirming and joyful memories, as well.

But things were not always smooth. There was one bright young doctoral student, for instance, who often appeared arrogant and dismissive of what I said or what transpired in class. She inconsiderately used her cell phone, missed classes, and did not take her listening sessions seriously. Small interventions did not change her behavior. Finally, I suggested that she drop the class. Her attitude was poor, her participation was superficial, and according to the class requirements, she was failing. I told her she could just withdraw, without a grade, so her GPA would not suffer.

Amazingly, she did not want to withdraw. I then told her if she stayed in the class and expected to pass, she must show a remarkable and definitive improvement in her attitude and output and have no more class absences. Moreover, she needed, with her listening partner, to participate in a weekly supervised listening session with me present. She agreed to all of these requirements with her partner's relieved endorsement and support.

The intervention was time-consuming, particularly the supervised listening sessions, which were two-and-a-half- to three-hour-long chunks of extra time each week. The added engagement allowed for this student to reflect on her self-protective, off-putting attitudes toward other people. Her outstanding personal work helped her to see there was a way to change the many years of chronic self-imposed but lonely isolation she had created around herself. The support of her caring partner, her class community, and my added guidance and supervision helped her begin a dramatic turn in behavior. Her movement was reflected in a private name change she suggested for herself at the end of the semester. In high school, she had named herself "Scorpion" to characterize her propensity to protect herself by hurting those who tried to get too close. At the end of our class, she claimed the name "Sunshine," a persona symbolizing a source of inviting warmth and light.

Friendship and Language Development

When I first arrived at NENU, I hoped to make good working connections with the faculty in the education and psychology departments. I wanted to get to know people, further my professional work, and find a comfortable place within the faculty. However, this was more difficult to do than I had thought. Everyone was busy. While people were very pleasant with me, I was shy, unclear on protocol, and clumsy about advocating for what I wanted. I also felt very limited by my Chinese illiteracy and low-level language proficiency. I did meet a wonderful dean whose office was near mine. When we first met, I was disarmed by his energy and charm. His minimal English fluency level was comparable to my minimal Chinese fluency. However, we somehow were able to communicate enough to become friends. He invited me out to eat, to visit his home, to meet his wife, to make dumplings. He seemed to enjoy my company for the social aspects, as I enjoyed his. When I once mentioned my interests to promote emotional literacy at NENU, he easily brushed the topic aside, preferring to "just be friends." He did not want to talk about work issues, and I didn't push the topic. Our friendship superseded my work goals.

Gratefully, through the foreign expert network, I did find myself a competent, engaging Chinese-language tutor, Helen, with whom I met twice weekly. She helped with my Chinese vocabulary, pronunciation, and conversation skills. She also educated me on various elements of Chinese behavior and culture that reminded me how similar yet different we were— she a Chinese native, I a Chinese-American. For half an hour of each lesson, Helen would tutor me in reading, pronunciation, and grammar. Then for the second half of the hour, we would converse in Chinese. Often, I would ask her questions about her life. She would respond, describing Chinese culture from her lived perspective, telling me how she grew up, her relationships with her mother and father, her schooling, her jobs, her challenges. She was engaging and funny, and we often ended up laughing together.

I also joined a Chinese/English language exchange that was started by a motivated group of young working professionals. Meeting times were Wednesday and Saturday evenings, and we gathered at a cozy coffeehouse a fifteen-minute walk from my residence. Occasionally, some of us would eat together before the meeting. Sometimes people would go elsewhere, afterward, for a beer. Often, when I was leaving these meetings, someone would walk me home. These walks home were friendly, where perhaps arm in arm, or hand in hand, more private conversations would ensue. In these circumstances, I felt like an auntie, an older sister, or a good buddy . . . nothing at all like a venerable Chinese-American scholar.

Being in China but illiterate and fairly inarticulate with the Chinese language was an ongoing challenge. I was happy and grateful to have found more times and places where I could practice and learn additional Chinese and, besides language practice, to be with people who were so much fun.

One evening early on, for example, I asked the people in my small group if they knew the classic poem "Lou Shi Ming" (陋室铭), "Inscription on a Crude Dwelling." Not missing a beat, one of the Chinese men named Chris confidently recited the poem. I was charmed by his recitation even after I found out that *all* children in China are required to learn and recite "Lou Shi Ming" when they are in middle school. Chris recited other poems that I didn't know and then told me he composed his own poems, too. He got embarrassed when asked to recite one of his own, but, with good-natured encouragement, he did. Then another participant, a visiting scholar from Russia named Ruslan, lightheartedly confessed that he too wrote poems and songs. In fact, he revealed, he composed music and led a band back home in Russia. Amid all this banter and merriment, I realized that learning Chinese and exchanging language skills in this group was going to be much more than just learning the language. It was also going to be about getting into each other's lives, building relationships, talking about genuine issues, enjoying lighthearted moments, and even getting through hard times together.

International Graduate Student Seminar and Offshoots

Besides my graduate class and my language exchange group, a third defining activity in my China Fulbright experience was the International Students Graduate Seminar. This seminar was first initiated in 1997 by Professor Zhu, a warm, intellectually generous, tenacious woman with impeccable English language fluency. The seminar, conducted in English, was held every Friday afternoon from 3:00 p.m. to 5:00 p.m. During this time, international graduate students[5] took turns explaining their academic research projects, presenting their thinking and questions, and writing drafts for critical feedback. Sometimes, professors were also invited to present their own ideas and research.

I was grateful to hear about this formal program and glad to be able to attend. It helped me know what students were doing around the university and gave me an opportunity to meet other colleagues and hear their ways of thinking and teaching. It also made me feel less isolated in my own academic life.

At one point, fortuitously, I was invited to present a lecture to this select group on emotional literacy. I was very relieved to receive this invitation because up until that point, I was not sure how to promote more interest in emotional literacy on campus. The talk was received quite positively. People's attention seemed fully engaged as I talked about emotional pain and healing. When I explained about one's innate ability to heal from past trauma and to reclaim healthy, positive relationships, I noticed some people were moved to tears. Afterward, participants came up to thank me for speaking or to ask more content questions. The positive feedback encouraged me to arrange subsequent workshops.

Simultaneously, I also invited a few friends and colleagues to have private peer counseling sessions with me. These sessions, where my partners and I shared uninterrupted speaking and listening time, modeled my class syllabus. The exercises were confidential sessions where partners talked, at will, about meaningful events, ideas, and feelings. In retrospect, I think these meetings could have been the groundwork for developing a more substantial emotional literacy program in Changchun. But there wasn't enough time. As it were, the sessions were unique opportunities to slow down, to take turns talking about what was important, to practice showing the depths of our feelings, and to benefit from being seen.

Off-Campus Workshops

I was invited to facilitate emotional literacy workshops in Zhuhai, Shenzhen, Beijing, and Shenyang. All these workshops and lectures focused on various aspects of listening skills, peer counseling, the acquiring of self-knowledge, and relationship and community building. As ever, new information seemed to be at the edges of participants' comfort levels and learning curves, but the audiences, predominately those in human services, were very receptive.

The last workshop I did, for the Public Affairs Section team at the US Consulate Office in Shenyang, was an example of this kind of receptivity. The Public Affairs Section head during my stay, Thanh, had heard me speaking informally about my work at a Fulbright-sponsored dinner. She was drawn to the idea of developing emotional literacy skills with her staff and asked me to do some final training with them, before her imminent departure back to the States. Thanh particularly wanted to strengthen her staff's sense of community, building trust between and among them. I gave her background material to explain my theoretical framework and approach. After vetting the material and further conversation, a date was determined, a schedule developed, and I found myself on a train to Shenyang just in time to attend the US Consulate's grand Fourth of July extravaganza.

In the consulate workshop the next day, Thanh's staff, all native Chinese women, were ready and open. It helped that these women knew and liked each other as well as trusted Thanh, their supervisor. They leaned into the exercises and through their personal sharing, moved to a new level of respect and understanding that could translate positively into their future work. Toward the end of the workshop, one of the women called the program "group therapy." It was hardly group therapy, but the shared stories were clearly therapeutic and community-building. It made me wonder at the possibilities of work that can happen when people dare to be genuine and honest with one another, past the politeness and separations that hierarchy and political correctness often impose.

Reviewing the Experience

Someone once mused that "We teach what we want to learn." For me, the phrase strikes true. It is so important to me to continue to learn and teach about emotional literacy. Human relations and communication skills are so personally valuable, life-saving, and life affirming. I think everyone should become familiar with them from a very young age. In China, I found an opportunity to build a working community of students who acquired some degree of success in learning about and practicing these skills. In the process, they helped disprove, at least for those of us involved, the cautionary tales that warn against trying to teach the stoic Chinese to talk and discuss feeling matters, both theirs and others. From my experiences with the students in my emotional literacy class, as well as throughout my other work in China, I re-affirmed my understanding that many native Chinese people are eager to learn about their feelings and emotional lives. They, as with other populations, Eastern and Western, just need a safe and trusting place to do this kind of exploration.

From exposure to the international student community, I was re-affirmed in my knowledge that all people have vulnerable feelings and cultures around what is permissible or non-permissible to express or discuss. But we, as feeling human beings, want to fully express ourselves whenever we can. The challenge is to make safe spaces that are comfortable enough to speak honestly, feel freely, and raise our thoughts without fear of negative consequences. Another challenge is to learn and practice the idea of being okay with discomfort and not running away from the unease that new ideas and the unfamiliar arouse. "Embrace the discomfort," I would encourage my audiences. "Let your feelings come up, whatever they are. Sit with them, breathe, and notice what they are telling you." I learned that people who practice these kinds of behaviors and self-reflective skills develop more sensitivity toward themselves as well as toward others.

Teaching emotional literacy concepts in China, I realized, was taking the broad goals of the Fulbright Program (to increase intercultural understanding in the hopes of promoting compassion, peace, and friendship)[6] and operationalizing them through practical skills. I encouraged people to keep giving each other chances and keep practicing trust despite the mistakes and betrayals (intentional or unwitting) that they had been subjected to. In this way, as William Fulbright also believed,[7] we can come to more peaceful, compassionate understandings of one another.

In China, I felt like I didn't have to prove my worth. Perhaps having been granted the position of "Fulbright scholar" was proof enough. Perhaps it was because I was unpretentious and tried to be kind. Perhaps it was, as some people told me, I reminded them of their beloved grandmother, mother, or auntie. Perhaps it was because I helped to stretch people's thinking and showed them new positive ways of looking at themselves and at the world when they were lost or confused. It's hard to say for sure. What it did for me, though, is make me feel solidly valued and secure.

My students looked out for me. They carried my backpack, invited me to eat with them, accompanied me to strange places, and translated for me. They patiently taught me Chinese. Other folks invited me into their homes, cooked for me, told me their secrets, and listened to some of mine. The friends I met in China (domestic and international) appreciated my teaching and my work and wanted to learn more. I traveled together with some of them to the border of North Korea and to the underground forest and foggy peaks at Chang Bai Shan. We composed songs, both silly and serious. We held hands, laughed, cried, and shared hugs together. In the end, I realized I had successfully formed the kind of caring community around myself that I had hoped to teach my students how to make for themselves, too. I felt so gratified.

On the day I was leaving Changchun, frenetic and harried, my Russian buddy, Ruslan, suggested we pause amid the last-minute busy-ness to sit quietly for a few minutes and just be with each other. And so, we did. He sat down on a side chair. I sat on a couch. Others sat or stood nearby. All these people, helping me to pack up, coming to spend just a little more time with me, coming to say farewell. An overwhelming sense of loss, gratitude, and love engulfed me, and I started to cry. I was leaving this beautiful city and these beautiful people, people who had invited me so generously into their lives and hearts. It ached. But the time was so well spent. Zai jian! Zai jian! Goodbye, Changchun! Zai jian.

Postscript

I left China, but China has not left me. I have invaluable memories, daily WeChat communications, ongoing international friendships, and present time academic collaborations. Unexpectedly, yet gratefully, I have realized a stronger sense of myself and a new sense of peace and centeredness regarding my teaching abilities. I am more confident. I have a better grasp of the knowledge that "less is more" and that it is okay to slow down, to take more time, to go deeper as opposed to broader, and to live and work in the present. I am more prepared to deal with the surprises that inevitably arise in my life and work. I am less inclined to take another person's negativity toward me as a personal failure. My successes in China buffer me against any mistreatment because I have repeatedly seen and experienced my competence and value reflected to me through the appreciation, love, and gratitude of those I have positively influenced. My Fulbright China experience re-confirms what I already knew: that no matter where we start, we strive to be in good relations with one another and that love is at the heart of everything.

Notes

1. Re-evaluation Counseling, RC, or "co-counseling" was developed by Harvey Jackins in the early 1950s. It's based on the idea that peers can help each other heal from emotional distress and reclaim the ability to think more clearly by taking turns talking about and discharging, or releasing, stored-up trauma and bottled-up emotions. See Harvey Jackins, *The Human Side of Human Beings* (Seattle: Rational Island Publishers, 1965). Print.
2. "Emotional Literacy" is the term coined by Claude Steiner. It is "the ability to be aware of, to feel, to understand and to use our emotions and the emotions of other people to the benefit of all involved." See Claude Steiner, *Achieving Emotional Literacy* (New York: William Morrow, 1997). Print.
3. Ibid.
4. I developed a series of ten lecture/workshops which I presented in Changchun, Zhuhai, Shenzhen, Beijing, and Shenyang. These workshops were invitations from friends and colleagues. The embassy workshop was the only event initiated by a connection through the Fulbright network.
5. The Chinese government gives full scholarships to students from developing countries (including room, board, travel, and living allowances) to study at universities throughout China, including at NENU.
6. "The Fulbright Program aims to bring a little more knowledge, a little more reason, and a little more compassion into world affairs and thereby to increase the chance that nations will learn at last to live in peace and friendship" (J. William Fulbright). Web. June 28, 2018.
7. Ibid.

9 Beijing Musings

On Rubbish Management, Masks, Local Delicacies, and Lecturing While Living as a Fulbrighter

Michael Fetters

Context as Distinguished Professor of the Social Sciences

I will start with a little bit of context. I served as Distinguished Chair in the Social Sciences at Peking University Health Sciences Center for the fall semester in 2016. At the time, the Distinguished Chair category involved teaching a graduate course, as well as conducting a research project. Like all Fulbrighters, I felt excitement and some trepidation about going. I felt particularly thrilled to receive the Fulbright support because I am a family physician, though I have long been interested in the social sciences, as I was an exchange student to Japan when I was 17 years old. Having majored in Japanese studies as an undergraduate while taking all the prerequisites to attend medical school, I benefitted from studies organized from constructivist and post-positivist views of the world. Throughout medical school and residency training, I always envisioned a future of cross-cultural work, though it was more of an ambience in my brain than a well-calculated plan.

Developing an Interest in China and Formative Experiences

The popular adage "All Asian Studies eventually lead to China" held true for me as well. As if studying medicine wasn't challenging enough, as a medical student, I took intensive Chinese language studies, the equivalent of a full year of Chinese, during one summer. This prepared me for a fourth-year medical student elective in Wuhan, famously known as one of the three ovens in China, at Tongji Medical School. Eager to take on a third language and culture, I participated in a two-month elective in my senior year of medical school. During this time, I studied, well . . . actually, mostly observed my teachers conducting acupuncture and prescribing traditional Chinese medicine. Just before leaving China in the spring of 1989, I visited Tiananmen Square with friends. Two weeks later, I watched from a world away in Ohio as the Tiananmen incident unfolded. My fledgling ember of interest in

China studies waned for decades in the aftermath until I had an opportunity for a sabbatical that I began planning in 2015. My dualistic undergraduate degree in Japanese studies combined with all the science and pre-medical education emblazoned both constructivist and post-positivist views of the world in my brain. My dialectically pluralistic self led me as a researcher to the use of mixed methods research as a family medicine researcher. Intent on returning to China, I developed a proposal that would involve conducting a project on cancer disclosure attitudes, while also teaching a mixed methods course.

Through the University of Michigan–Peking University Health Sciences Center collaborative platform, I had the pleasure and honor of meeting Professor Cong Yali, a medical ethicist from Peking University Health Sciences Center, who welcomed me to teach. My intent through the following observations is to provide some stories that have what I believe to be practical advice stir fried with a light sauce of humor. Almost assuredly my lens as a family physician and social scientist drove my curiosity about environmental issues, masks, and gastronomics.

Lesson on How to Get Things Done: Cleaning Up the Courtyard

When I first arrived at my apartment complex, I was a bit taken aback. As I was living on a major university campus, one of the top universities in China, I thought the housing would be a little more upscale than usual. I am not sure what I expected, but I wasn't prepared for what really caught my eyes as I arrived at my new home for the first time. There were three tall buildings that formed a U shape, and they were peeling paint and supporting rather rusted massive letters bearing the name for the apartment complex. There was a fence around the area and a guardhouse by the main gate. I am not actually sure what the guards did beyond smoke cigarettes, eat, and watch TV, as these were the only activities I ever observed them engage in.

At any rate, when I walked through the entry gate for the first time, there was courtyard bordered by three buildings that formed the enclosed residential area, and I later learned that the big sign on the top of the building gave this complex its name, the "Youth Compound." While it may have served youth at one time, it appeared the buildings had aged with them. A guardhouse at the entrance to the street and, by extension, a fence formed the fourth wall of a square courtyard. As I walked into the compound area, I noticed a weedy, almost grassy area in the middle, which was overgrown. The overflowing and malodorous trash bins aside, something else caught my eye. It was the amount of rubbish and discarded, no longer-usable items. There were three old toilets, yes, the tank and the commode. There was a love seat next to an apartment entrance that it appeared someone was using, as it wasn't wet from rain (not a common occurrence in Beijing). There were two cloth armchairs, both just dumped upside down. There were two mattresses contorted like a Gumby toy scattered about. All were obviously collecting moisture in the shaded area of the courtyard, and they almost assuredly harbored a sundry of critters. There was a kitchen cabinet that had clearly been cut from the furnishing chopping block occupying another corner of the area. In addition, there were large plastic bins that seemed to be overflowing with rotten or overly ripe vegetables. I thought, "I am here by choice and I *could* get used to this."

For three days, I couldn't help but commiserate about the dumping grounds in my courtyard every time I came in or out of the apartment compound. Four days after I arrived, I was walking back to my apartment from work and noticed a Chinese woman precariously pushing a love seat on an impossibly undersized pushcart. It looked like the cart was from a research lab for moving trays and other apparatus. The love seat was up-ended so it wobbled side to side with each small crack, bump, or rock. As I walked up from behind, the woman was struggling to push the undersized cart as the love seat keep vacillating from side to side. What made it all the more entertaining was that the woman was quite petite, even for Chinese standards.

Convinced that she needed a hand, I said, "*Nihao!*" ("Hello!") And she looked a little surprised that I, a foreigner, had greeted her.

She replied back in perfect English, "Oh, hello."

I offered to assist her, and she declined (the usual routine for any offer of help) but finally succumbed. As we slowly walked, pushed the cart over bumpy spots on the road, and talked, I informed her that I was a Fulbright scholar staying on the campus. She said she had just returned from conducting research in Boston, and she was moving this love seat into her house. At this point, we had waddled along around 150 meters, and we reached the entrance to my compound. She lived in the same compound. So, we pushed the love seat through the gate and started moving through the courtyard.

As we entered the courtyard, I looked at her and then cast a glance from side to side. I then told her with a subdued grin, "If you need any more furniture, you can get some for free here in the courtyard."

She looked at me with contempt and replied, "I hate these things here."

In response, I added, "Yeah, this is a great place for rats and snakes." She looked back at me and shook her head with a complex non-verbal facial contortion composed of fear, fright, and disgust. I said, "Maybe someone should call to have these things removed."

We reached the entryway to her apartment stairs, and I offered to help move it into her apartment, but she declined, stating she had family to help. So, we departed with her love seat a Leaning Tower of Pisa, perched and dwarfing the pushcart parked by the building entrance. She disappeared into her stairwell in a whirlwind. Feeling happy to have met one of my new neighbors and believing I had done a good deed sprinkled with a sense of humor, I retired for the evening.

The next day, I departed as usual and went off to work with my usual morning sendoff from the commodes, armchairs, and mattresses. When I returned that evening, to my surprise, low and behold, the three toilets, the two chairs, the kitchen cabinet, and the mattresses were all *gone*! I couldn't believe my eyes.

Now, I suppose one must be careful in surmising cause and effect, but it does seem that the mere mention of rats and snakes was effective. Even though she was my neighbor, I never saw her again, not even once. But I think she was by far one of my best neighbors ever! So, I learned that the best way to get things done may not be by trying to accomplish it on your own but through friends however precariously you meet. So, if you are facing what seems like an intractable situation, remember to remind yourself, "I get by with a little help from my friends!"

Lessons on Why to Wear a Mask: More Than Mitigates the Microns

Masks and 2.5 Microns

For most casual observers, the reason one wears a mask in China is obvious—that is, to filter out the 2.5μm particles that are unhealthy. These tiny pollutants are the source of premature aging and severe morbidity and mortality. Air and water pollution in major Chinese cities is a serious issue. Known as *wumai*, the air pollution is a common topic of complaint and misgiving among the Chinese. Indeed, my graduate student told me the best days in Beijing were days that were windy or raining since these helped to clear away the *wumai*. Complaining about *wumai* commonly comes up as a topic of discussion, but the average Beijinger can do little about it other than wear a mask and hope for rainy days.[1]

Masks have additional important functions. Masks can not only keep foul particles and smells out but keep warmth in. A mask helps keep hold the heat on your cheeks on the cold, blustery days when you are walking to the subway station, fighting gusty winds. Masks can also protect the user from the germs generated by the 22 million Beijingers in the capital city. The corollary is wearing a mask makes you an advocate for public health, as it can keep your own germs in.

Now the downsides of masks are not to be ignored. One of the most annoying is the way glasses fog up when the moisture from your exhalation pushes around the upper edges of your mask and clouds up the lenses. Another is when rubber straps irritate your ears or tangle in your hair. Beware of the knockoffs. Rumor has it that there are numerous fake masks in Beijing, those lacking the real capacity for mitigating the 2.5 micron particles. So, if you find them cheap, check them carefully, and perhaps be content wearing them for warmth and for germ gating. So, open up the package, and don't just reserve your mask for poor air quality days. There's more to masks than mitigating microns.

Lessons for the Palate: Culinary Quips

Nowhere in the world is it clearer that "food is culture" than in China. I heard this from so many people in different places, and it is so true—going to a restaurant with a number of friends and then poring over the menu to see what dishes are there and listening to exchanges back and forth about what is good and what is in season, how it will go with this, how it will go with that, how to keep balance among the different dishes, and of course, which soup to get, because there has to be soup. I have never witnessed waiters or waitresses to be as patient as in China. When they come to take your order, there seems to be no real rush. Sometimes I have even wondered if it is the closest they get to a break. Ordering food and getting it just as you want is sacred. Depending on their own mood, they may be more or less helpful. But they almost always seem to be patient. Because choosing well, and eating well, is a ritual that is sacred. But beware—it wasn't long before I learned *not* to trust my intuition or pictures. I never seemed to choose very good dishes compared to my friends and colleagues who batted around the options until they inevitably arrived at good choices, minus one or two. There is strength in numbers, so ordering multiple dishes does provide a buffer against the almost inevitable questionable selection.

Don't Be a Clean Plater

The variety of foods that can be eaten in China is unequivocally remarkable. Chinese food is the most diverse food in the world and claims to be the most _____ (fill in the blank with an adjective of your choosing, e.g., colorful, filling, fattening, and so on). Nonetheless, the most _____ does not always mean the most tasteful or the most masticable. Though I grew up conditioned to be a clean plater in Central Ohio, this is not such a good idea in Beijing. Chinese cooking was developed with a combination of ingredients intended for consumption and ingredients chosen to add flavor that are not to be eaten but spit out, as frequently happens.

First exhibit for not being a clean plater. If you order meat dishes, then you will find bones or other in unpalatable objects in virtually any dish served. Animal bones, especially long bones, have bone marrow, a substance that has many healthy properties. Leaving bones in can help minimize wasted meat that can occur from cutting them out and throwing them away with small scraps of meat still clinging. Moreover, the bones, when cooked, add a lot of flavor, but they are very crunchy, a little too crunchy for most. If you eat fish, you will find bones in virtually any dish served. If you eat pork, you will find bones in virtually any dish served, and if you eat chicken, you will find bones, yep, in virtually any dish you get. While I am an avid carnivore, my friend and fellow Fulbrighter J.J. frequently reminded me she was never so happy to be a vegetarian as when living in China. I suppose she has a point. In short, for whatever the rationale, assume your meat dishes have bones.

Pass on the Perilous Peppers

Second exhibit. Take the colorful and potent red chili peppers. These are nearly ubiquitous in certain regions of China, e.g., Szechuan, Chongqing, Hunan, the usual suspects. And there is another type of hot pepper (capsaicin) that will numb your tongue, lips, and anything else it comes into contact with. This pepper is actually the active ingredient in a topical arthritis medication with the same name. These little power packs of flavor can often be lurking in bites when you least expect them, and they take on the appearance of sauces and other ingredients as the food is flash cooked.

When my family visited and I took them to a cooking class with Chef Zhou in his home as part of a culinary tour, he explained how he loved the way the capsaicin pepper caused his lips to tingle and how this made the perfect combination with a nice cold beer. I am not one to disagree with a professional chef, especially Chef Zhou, particularly about the cold beer. Bear in mind, you have a choice as to whether, and how much, you want your lips and mouth to be numb. Remember, don't swallow the peppers. But if you do, be prepared to pay the piper![2]

On Being a Good Guest

Third exhibit. In the West, manners mean being a clean plater, but if your plate is empty, this sends the wrong message to your host over dinner. In China, if your plate is empty, then it sends a signal that you are still hungry. Now actually, I have yet to go to a social gathering of friends where there wasn't more food than anyone could eat, but should it be the case where there is relatively little left, do not endeavor to finish. It will encourage your host to order more food!

On Finding the Best Peking Duck in Peking

In the course of lecturing in the year prior to my Fulbright, I visited China with my close colleague John W. Creswell. John is a prolific writer and leading author on qualitative and mixed methods research. As we were scheduled for several high-profile visits at top universities, we naturally were invited to celebrate our workshop success with our hosts over a meal. Dr. Creswell made it known that he loved Peking duck. After our workshop at the first institution, we were told we were heading to eat Peking duck at *the* best Peking duck restaurant in Peking and, of course, by default, the world. As we went to dinner with our friends, indeed we visited a restaurant serving Peking duck, and it was clearly very famous, as there were praises of the duck to be found on the walls, with posters of famous Chinese leaders, and there was Peking duck on every table. It was a very nice meal.

Two days later, we visited another prestigious university. Again, it was no secret that my colleague John very much liked Peking duck. As we finished off the workshop at the end of the day, our very kind hosts told us excitedly that we were having Peking duck for dinner and the restaurant we were headed for served *the* best Peking duck in Peking. We weren't certain if this meant we were headed to the same restaurant or not, but when we clambered out of our car, we saw we had arrived at a different location. It was an area surrounded by large buildings and people in every direction. I recall moving up the stairs into a very crowded restaurant. As we headed inside, the claims of it having the best Peking duck were everywhere to be found, and there was Peking duck to be found on every table. We enjoyed another evening of excellent Peking duck.

Now, this was quite the lecture circuit that had been arranged, so two days later, we were providing another mixed methods workshop at another top institution. In honor of our presentation, our hosts invited us to an evening meal to celebrate, and we were told with great enthusiasm that we were headed to a restaurant with *the* best Peking duck in Peking! As we arrived, we found large signage indicating that Chairman Mao had eaten at this restaurant and proclaimed it the best Peking duck in China. Personally, I was starting to have my fill of Peking duck, but I must admit that it still was quite good.

Fast forward a year to the closing days of my fall semester as a Fulbright scholar. While in China, I had eaten Peking duck on several occasions but accompanied with a claim of it being the best. Then, on Christmas Eve, one of my colleagues who had lived in the UK was very kind and invited me to join her family for a dinner and an evening show with them. She then told me they had selected on this special occasion a restaurant serving . . . Peking duck! We rode to a restaurant, and I felt I had grown close to them as friends, close enough I could tell them my story of having the *best* Peking duck on three different nights in three different restaurants the year before. She and her husband laughed. She said, "Well, maybe where we are going to today is not the best, but it is very good." When all the crispy skin, slices of thin cucumber, and delicate wraps were gone, I decided they were right; it was very good, in fact better than all the other three! It made me realize that the best Peking duck is more about the company than the crispy skin.

On Dealing with a Call From the Beijing National Security Office

As a Fulbrighter, one of the really wonderful perks is the traveling lecture program. Early in the semester, the Fulbright office puts out a request for topics you are willing to lecture about in other universities, and then these topics are delivered to Chinese universities throughout China. Under this arrangement, Fulbright reimburses for the travel costs and the host institution pays for meals and lodging. Visiting professors are encouraged to prepare a little information about their background and introduce the speakers to US culture. It is a great program, and I started off with a trip to the beautiful city of Xiamen. With it being my first trip, I was a little nervous, having only recently completed our orientation where there had been an emphasis on being vigilant about registering with the local authorities wherever we traveled. It was never quite clear though if this meant anywhere you traveled, if you were going for a very short stay, or only if you were planning to live there a while. I subsequently learned that hotels are supposed to do this, and if they don't, it is because the local police don't care. After arriving and lecturing twice in Xiamen with only one more to go, I was feeling as though it was all working out. Then, my second afternoon there, I receive a phone call on my Chinese smartphone from a Beijing number. Naturally, I was eager to talk with anyone back in Beijing who wanted to talk with me, so I answered. I was asked in English, "Is this Michael Fetters?"

"Yes, who is calling?" I answered.

The caller said, "I am Wang Jing[3] from the National Security Office, Beijing Branch. I want to come and visit your office to talk with you."

Now, of course I was surprised to hear I was being called by what I perceived to be the equivalent of the CIA and was a little anxious.

I replied, "I am sorry, but I am in Xiamen." [Thought: maybe I wasn't registered after all, and I am in trouble. Maybe I should be careful what information I disclose.] "I will not be back in Beijing until Thursday."

"Okay, I will come to your office on Thursday at 11:00 a.m."

I called my Fulbright contact immediately, and we discussed the issue. She explained this was not uncommon. Part of the job of the National Security Office is to go around and meet foreigners residing in China. She explained that they just come and talk with you and ask some questions. "Easy for you to say," I thought to myself. But I trusted her advice and tried not to get too worked up about the visit.

At the anointed time of 11:00 a.m., not just one, but two National Security Office, Beijing Branch, officers showed up. I was surprised because they were dressed in street clothes, jeans, a blouse, and light jacket for the younger woman and dressier pants and a button-up collar shirt on the man. Undercover agents! I introduced myself and asked if they were from the national office. They said yes, and I requested IDs. They pulled a leather flip case, and sure enough, there was a bright shiny badge inside. The woman was clearly more accomplished in English than the senior male agent.

She took the lead and said they were there to ask some routine questions about my background. (Sigh of relief, as that was what my Fulbright contact had advised, whew!) I am not sure what came over me, some kind of crazy ambition or a fight-or-flight response, but I decided it might be better to conduct this discussion in my fledgling Chinese. Now, while this may portend well for ongoing language skill development, it honestly makes following completely what they had to say more difficult.

On the spur of the moment, I thought, "If I am going to wing this in Chinese, it would be easiest to use the slide presentation I made for the traveling lecture program." So, I told them, "I have a PPT (pronounced in Chinese, pee pee tee) about my background. Would you like to see it?"

They said that would be fine.

Now, in this slide set, I have pictures of Michigan, my home, my front and backyard, my four sons, and especially fishing pictures. I began using pictures to explain what state I was from (Ohio), where I attended undergraduate, medical school, and graduate school (twice). I showed a slide of my wife relaxing and a photo of her in her white coat as a professor. I showed a picture of my oldest son playing soccer, my second son blowing out birthday candles, and my third son catching a fish. Finally, I showed a picture of my fourth son blowing snow in winter and cutting grass in summer. I then explained I was to teach a course of mixed methods research. As I was chatting away, feeling they must surely be enjoying learning about a real American, I noticed that the senior person was gazing at his watch. It was already 11:30 a.m., which meant that the time-honored hour of lunch was approaching. Some non-verbal communication patterns are universal, so I rushed through a final slide, feeling as though I had just delivered my first lecture in Chinese, and shut down my computer.

As the flip top of my computer snapped to a close, I peered up to look for their responses, and we cast gazes from person to person in a protracted moment of silence. The senior officer then spoke in accented but completely comprehensible English, "You are truly professor!" We all laughed, and with that, they scurried off. I stopped to pause in the exhilaration that I had just survived a half an hour of interrogation by the Beijing Branch of the National Security Office—or perhaps lectured for a half an hour in Chinese. I had unequivocally proved to them I was who I said, in Chinese. Apparently, these visits are not too uncommon, so don't be surprised if you get a call. I am not sure if I was putting them to sleep or torturing them with my Chinese or if it was just me between them and their lunch. I can't speak for whether or not it will help you but taking control of the conversation worked for me!

Reflections: Lessons Learned

These reflections echo the theme of the book: flow like water. Many surprises await the Fulbright scholar. I strongly vouch for more than a short stay. Of course, there are many rewards of developing friendships, but one is its effectiveness of getting things done. Indeed, I found myself at the end of the semester wishing I could have stayed longer, a sentiment I hear from most who go for the short haul. These observations and reflections for me illustrate how curiosity and an attitude injected with a little humor and confidence can lead you, or perhaps sustain you, as you meander through what will be one of the most memorable moments in your life.

Notes

1. Editor's note: It is a common misconception that rain significantly reduces Beijing air pollution. In fact, wind is the primary factor in clearing the air. See the website by Fulbright alumnus Thomas Thalem, founder of SmartAir. Choon Khin, "You Thought Rain Washes Away Pollution?" *Smart Air Filters Blog Post*, June 20, 2017. Web. December 18, 2018.
2. Editor's note: Szechuan flower peppers cause mouth numbing and lip tingling. They are not related to chili peppers and do not contain capsaicin.
3. A pseudonym.

10 Experiencing Urban Infrastructure in Tianjin

Jonathan Ochshorn

Introduction

China has embarked on a program of infrastructure construction that has transformed its urban centers to a remarkable extent, especially over the last two or three decades. Cars, taxis, busses, roads, and highways; subways, high-speed trains, and railway terminals; planes and airports; along with all sorts of other public amenities, from shopping malls to public toilets, have radically altered the experience of living in, and traveling between, Chinese cities. Based on observations made during a five-month teaching appointment in Tianjin—a sprawling port city of fifteen million people just southeast of Beijing—this chapter recounts infrastructural adventures that I experienced as a US architect and teacher with no Chinese language skills but with a strong desire to explore this rapidly developing urban territory.

Infrastructure is here used in a broad sense, encompassing not only the state-run urban and interurban transport systems that support the expanding economy but also other systems that, even when organized by private capital, provide a similarly systemic underpinning for the requirements of daily life in Tianjin.

Housing Infrastructure

After our Fulbright orientation in Beijing, I am driven with my wife, Susan, to the nearby city of Tianjin with six pieces of luggage and two boxes of books. Beijing and Tianjin are literally contiguous (with a smaller city, Lang-fang, interrupting what would otherwise be a more consistently continuous border), yet the experience of driving from Beijing to Tianjin feels more like leaving one city, traveling through mile after mile of non-urbanized land, and then finally entering what feels like another city. In other words, while the political boundaries of the cities are enormous, the actual urban-ized areas within those boundaries are quite a bit smaller. Between those urbanized areas are large zones of agricultural land, interspersed with small, dense settlements containing row after row of repetitive walk-up, multi-story, south-facing apartment blocks. As we enter the more urbanized area of Tianjin, some buildings get taller, a few begin to stand out because of their unique form, and we exit the highway, driving the last few miles on a more conventional grid of urban streets.

We drop off our boxes at the School of Architecture and then drop off our luggage at our nearby campus apartment on the third floor of a six-floor walk-up for foreign scholars, the apartment block being similar to the south-facing units that we passed on our drive from Beijing. Each bar-like housing block has a front and a back facade, with the southern exposure being most valued. For that reason, the spaces, or streets, between the housing blocks are not at all symmetrical, as they often are in Western residential districts. In a typical suburban or urban street in the US, for example, one would expect to find entrances to dwelling units or apartments on both sides of the street, irrespective of their solar orientation. Here, however, as we drive east down the "street" between the apartment blocks, all the entrances are on our right, that is, on the northern facade. On the left, or southern facade, we see an array of fenced-in backyards for the first-floor units, sometimes with roofs and walls enclosing the yard and creating an extra ground-level room. Between the two apartment blocks are parking spaces, some of which, toward the northern facade, are covered with corrugated steel panels supported on lightweight steel frames.

The southern, sun-facing side of each apartment contains a large balcony, often enclosed in glass, where occupants can hang up their laundry to dry. In our apartment, this balcony is accessed from the master bedroom; we also have a closed-in balcony on the northern facade that contains a small two-burner gas stove (but no oven) adjacent to the kitchen. In other words, our apartment spans from north to south, allowing through-circulation of air—something difficult to accomplish in apartment arrangements where a double-loaded corridor, typically connected to fire stairs and elevators, splits the slab into two distinct zones. We, of course, have neither an elevator (I did say "walk-up") nor a corridor but rather a single stair at the northern entry that serves three apartments on each of the six floors. Several of these six-story, eighteen-unit modules are then placed side by side to create a block-long slab with multiple north-facing entrances, each with its own stair.

From my standpoint, this low-rise apartment block design, repeated thousands of times in Chinese cities, has both positive and negative qualities. On the plus side, the consistent attention to solar orientation is extremely valuable, especially if you are air-drying laundry but also just to guarantee that each apartment will have direct access to a good deal of sunshine.

Two-thirds of the apartments, including our own, also have a northern exposure, which promotes air circulation. This benefit becomes merely "theoretical," however, when the outdoor air quality reaches an unhealthy level, which turns out to be quite often, and windows remain shut. The walk-up stair is good (lots of exercise) and bad (too much climbing, especially if you are feeling ill or otherwise incapacitated); we are placed in a third-floor apartment, which is high enough above the ground to feel relatively secure and quiet but not so high as to feel oppressive.

On the negative side, the relentless differentiation between north and south facades creates a building with an unimpeachable internal logic *as a building* but with much less success in creating a viable social space within the streets between building blocks. In some cultures, it is the street, rather than any individual building, that determines the identity of what might be called home ground, and it is primarily the design and functionality of building facades that *create* the space of the street. Where the street-building interfaces on *both* sides of the street support semi-private zones of entry stairs, stoops, porches, or small yards, the spatial and social reading of the street becomes even more complex and far richer. From this type of street, one not only *sees* buildings on each side but can also access those buildings.

In contrast to this model, the pattern of streets within my residential district in Tianjin is merely the utilitarian outcome of design decisions that have only considered the logic of the building itself as a self-contained entity—the street merely serves as a mode of access and a location for parking. Each street is almost literally bisected into two strips, the northern side with its private yards and the southern, more public, side given over to parking and entrances for a different housing block. In such a street, the northern edge is walled off and often inaccessible, except perhaps for the ground-floor apartments, which partake of a schizophrenic existence—connected via a public entrance on a different street further north down the block while having a private yard facing another building's public entrances across to the south.

To be fair, my critique is a bit idealistic and somewhat hypocritical, in that it presumes that the contrasting "Western" model, where the street is intended to foster a sense of community, is more than a nostalgic relic from a bygone day. Even in the "New Urbanist" model city of Seaside, Florida, where street-facing porches are mandated in the town's design guidelines to encourage precisely this type of street-centered community, the residents' behavior doesn't correspond to the architects' and planners' vision. Instead, people "seldom sit out on the porches so the social function for which they were designed (that is, to keep eyes on the street and as a place from which to greet passersby) has not really been realized."[1] The truth is that this apparent lack of community-oriented public space is more a function of changing lifestyles—in which *both* parents are at work all day, children's "free time" is largely organized for them in structured (i.e., *not* in the street) activities, and village-based multi-generational extended families have become increasingly obsolete in the wake of rapid urbanization—than because of any particular design strategies invoked, whether in US or Chinese cities.

Multi-story walk-up apartment blocks are the prevalent housing type in Tianjin, but there are also high-rise residential towers and older low-rise apartment buildings that have a more traditional relationship to the grid of streets. Based on a Tianjin master plan,[2] Zhang and Brown estimated that the overwhelming majority (80%) of housing in Tianjin takes the form of multi-story walk-up apartment blocks, much like the one we are living in near the university, with the rest split fairly equally between high-rise and low-rise buildings. My impression is that since this study was written, a greater percentage of current housing in Tianjin is being constructed as high-rise units. These percentages appear to be an artifact of large-scale demolition of traditional low-rise housing, in so-called *Hutong* districts, that has occurred within the recent past. One urban blogger[3] investigated "before" and "after" satellite images from Google Earth and concluded that

> between November 2000 and January 2004 almost the entirety of the area within the old city walls [of Tianjin] . . . and a considerable part of historic districts outside the walls, was destroyed. Apart from a couple of important temples, hardly a building escaped the destruction. Between 2004 and 2009 the entire area was rebuilt primarily with high-rise residential buildings and a grid of large wide avenues.

This is especially remarkable because, according to Campanella, "Chinese cities entered a kind of urban architectural time warp during the Cultural Revolution. . . . Most cities experienced almost no physical expansion in this period."[4] It was only during the fifteen years of rebuilding after the Tangshan earthquake of 1976[5] continuing with the radical economic and urban expansion of the twenty-first century—including the government's "massive capital injection amounting to 4 trillion yuan (approximately $586 billion US)" in response to the economic crisis of 2008[6]—that a large percentage of the traditional *Hutong* districts were demolished and replaced with six-story walk-up blocks and high-rise towers. Susan and I later walk through the old city district and down the nearby "Ancient Culture Street," where we buy some art supplies; all of the recently demolished storefronts, I now realize, have been reconstructed in a homogeneous, bland, but vaguely "ancient" (and not entirely unpleasant) style.

It is easy to criticize the demolition of these *Hutong* districts, using the same sort of arguments about "community" or architectural heritage that still inform debates about the preservation of neighborhoods in both developed and developing nations. However, as Campanella argues after extolling the "humanistic urbanism" exemplified by the *Hutong* districts of Beijing:

> Of course, it is easy to be seduced by all this, especially as a foreigner who has never had to spend a cold winter night in an old hutong flat heated, if at all, by a tiny coal stove. It might make for good urbanism, but most housing in these old neighborhoods was terribly overcrowded, unsanitary, and unsafe. Decades of deferred maintenance took a heavy toll on the structures, and many units lacked running water, a kitchen, or private bathroom. . . . The very real need to upgrade housing combined with the emergence of a real estate market and the ensuing development binge spelled its doom.[7]

Transportation Infrastructure

Our first experience with Tianjin's transportation infrastructure takes place in taxis, which roam the streets searching for curbside customers, but can also be "ordered" through smartphone applications, especially the "Swiss-army-knife" (i.e., does everything) social media mega-application called WeChat. With WeChat, one can both call and pay for taxis using software coordinated with the Uber-killing Didi Chuxing organization, which has apparently become the dominant ride-hailing application in China. I use the word *apparently*, because I spend my five months in China without a smartphone and therefore am only marginally aware of the actual source of taxis that seem to appear magically when summoned by various friends or colleagues. For example, immediately after our *waiban* takes us to lunch at a campus restaurant, she orders a taxi to take us to Carrefour, the French megastore, for some basic household food and supplies. (*waiban* is a contraction of *Waishi banchu*, or Foreign Affairs Office, and is the informal title given to the person assigned by Tianjin University to take care of us.)

As it turns out, the appearance of these taxis takes place in the immediate aftermath of two huge, and consequential, taxi wars. The first, between 2012 and 2015, pitted two Chinese companies against each other, both seeking to dominate the emerging ride-hailing market:

> They [the two rivals] provided subsidies to service providers and sent online coupons to millions of potential patrons. They fronted so much money to both providers and users of the service that the market knew that this was not sustainable, even though both companies had deep-pocketed financial backing. In 2015, the investors for the two companies came together and facilitated their merger. The merged company carried the name of Didi Chuxing.[8]

The second battle began when Uber, the San Francisco–based transportation company, made an aggressive move into the Chinese market in 2014, while its two Chinese rivals were still battling each other for market share. Uber's strategy ultimately failed, although the merger of Uber China with Didi Chuxing was not exactly a financial blow for Uber. Manjoo reports that the "$2 billion Uber spent tackling China is now worth about $7 billion in the new merged entity."[9]

Uber's decision to sell its Chinese operations to Didi Chuxing was announced in August 2016, just weeks before we arrive in China. Yet I can't help thinking of a similar transfer of Western sovereignty to China that occurred nineteen years earlier when the United Kingdom formally "handed over" Hong Kong. Much like our arrival in China just weeks after the Uber China merger, Susan and I arrived in Hong Kong just weeks after its return to Chinese sovereignty in July 1997. At that time, I began a one-year teaching appointment at the Chinese University of Hong Kong, which, unlike my current appointment in Tianjin, was not connected with the Fulbright Program.

Even if the impact and significance of the Uber-Didi merger and the Hong Kong Handover cannot really be equated, the two events nevertheless effectively bracket and highlight two decades of radical change in the relationship between China and the West. And such an equation may not actually be that far-fetched. Manjoo, for example, argues that "Uber's deal with Didi . . . points to [a] series of accommodationist deals in which giants cede large parts of the world to one another, pragmatically carving out their spheres of influence like players in The Great Game."[10] From this standpoint, battles to control the emerging digital, Internet-based infrastructure underlying markets in areas such as commerce (Amazon vs. Alibaba), search (Google vs. Baidu), social media (Facebook vs. WeChat), and transportation (Uber vs. Didi) may well be comparable in importance to prior (and current) battles for sovereignty over, or access to, physical territory. It is no accident that these battles to control *digital* infrastructure coincide with China's One Belt, One Road Initiative, which seeks to develop an expanded global *physical* transportation infrastructure.[11]

In spite of the enormous investment in transportation infrastructure in Chinese cities, such as Tianjin, our primary means of locomotion is walking. Susan and I are inclined by both temperament and habit to explore cities on foot, but to do this effectively requires at least some idea about potential destinations, whether those destinations are specific parks, buildings, monuments, or even entire districts. I am not interested in simply walking out of our apartment and blindly heading off in some arbitrary direction; for one thing, we will need to find our way back home, and, at least at first, I have no confidence in our ability to communicate with others should we get lost.

So finding a map is a prerequisite to any pedestrian adventure. Knowing that Google Maps would be blocked in China, I have taken the precaution, before leaving the US, of screen-capturing perhaps two dozen detailed portions of the Google map of Tianjin centered around the university and extending several miles in all directions, and I splice them together into one enormous image, which I load into my laptop and take with me. By zooming in, I can identify street names in "English" (actually, what appears to be English is really a form of pinyin—a transcription of Chinese sounds using the Roman alphabet—but without diacritic markings for tones), as well as the identity of selected buildings, rivers, and even subways. It's not clear how accurate this map is, but it proves to be extremely useful, since virtually all the information I can find online, once I am in Tianjin, is entirely in Mandarin. It is only later that Susan and I discover a map application provided by Apple, which I can download onto my iPod Touch (and which Susan can access on her iPhone), providing fairly good maps and directions in English.

I still can't figure out which destinations are worth exploring: Are there districts within the city with unique characteristics or important landmarks? Our maps do not provide much guidance, but various travel guides give us at least a sense of the internal districts and their relationship to Tianjin's history. The Heping district seems to have several attractions, being not only the site of the former British, French, and Japanese concessions but also home to upscale shopping malls, office buildings, and hotels.

With our hand-drawn map, Susan and I begin walking through the campus of Tianjin University, along interconnected water bodies that seem to retain some memory of a more natural state. In fact, when part of the pond is drained in order to repair a pavilion at the edge of the water, I can see that what looks like a "pool" actually has no shallow concrete bottom but rather is quite deep and muddy. As Susan and I walk east, we see a few older men sitting on the southern edge of the ponds casting their fishing rods into the water (though it's not clear if they intend to actually catch anything).

Continuing along Nanjing Road, we encounter our first glimpse of a more upscale and modern commercial environment populated with large buildings, flashing lights, and serious urban traffic. But we miss the left turn into the former British Concession that's marked on our hand-drawn map and walk a bit farther along Nanjing Road, ending up at the "Resists Earthquakes Monument," a heroic edifice consisting of a hollowed out stone pyramid with monumental sculptures of human figures in each of four quadrants.

The quake that has been memorialized here, one of the deadliest in human history, originated in the neighboring city of Tangshan in 1976, killing hundreds of thousands of people there, as well as over twenty thousand in Tianjin alone.[12] After returning to the US, I read a geological study that examines historic seismic activity along the Tangshan-Hejian-Cixian fault zone—the same fault implicated in the disastrous Tangshan earthquake of 1976.[13] The report concludes that a 100-mile-long seismic gap directly under Tianjin appears to be still holding back eight thousand years of accumulated and unreleased tectonic energy that could slip at any moment (any moment, that is, within the next two thousand years), causing a magnitude 7.5 earthquake centered in Tianjin. Although I have an adventurous spirit, my tolerance for risk is low, and I'm happy to have discovered this new information *after* returning home.

Toward the end of our stay in China, I take the subway back from Tianjin's South Railway Station and get off at the stop nearest to my apartment, still about two miles from home. I decide to extend the walk just a bit by stopping at a French bakery that has been recommended by a French expat Susan and I met some time before. I then walk home with two baguettes and make myself a cabbage-onion omelet, which I eat with the baguette, butter, and some cucumber slices. Meanwhile, Susan is out with our across-the-hall neighbor, getting her first Tianjin foot massage. She sends me a WeChat photo pointing down at her soaking feet.

Reflections

In this chapter, I have focused mostly on *hard* infrastructural elements like housing and transport systems, but China's educational system, a component of the so-called *soft* infrastructure "necessary for the maintenance of economic, health, cultural, and social standards"[14] also engages my attention while lecturing about US practice in the areas of building technology and sustainability. The importance of, and contradictory impulses within, soft infrastructure can be seen in the persistence of traditional Chinese culture, harnessed to preserve "such traditional virtues . . . as patriotism, respect for law, courtesy, integrity, solidarity, diligence and frugality" in order to counteract any potentially disruptive influences arising from China's move toward a market economy.[15] I think about two examples from my own experience with China's modern educational infrastructure in relation to traditional Chinese culture: one involving seminar instruction and the other involving so-called linguistic instrumentalism.

In the first case, the persistence of traditional Chinese culture can be seen in the apparent reticence of Chinese students to speak out in class.[16] This concerns me since I intend to offer one of my courses in a seminar format, in which class discussion is a key pedagogic element. When I taught architecture students at the Chinese University of Hong Kong just after the "Handover" to Chinese sovereignty in 1997—and in spite of explicit American influence on the department's curricular design along with an engrained British colonial influence—behaviors rooted in traditional Chinese culture that tended to inhibit discussion were nevertheless present. Tunney Lee, the founding chair of the architecture department there and former head of the Department of Urban Studies and Planning at MIT, tested various strategies in an attempt to overcome these tendencies, e.g., interrupting the flow of a lecture by having small groups of students caucus together and, *as a group*, pose questions or formulate responses.

Gu Mingyuan, a noted Chinese scholar in the field of comparative education, suggests that while traditional Chinese culture easily adapted to certain teaching methods imported from the Soviet Union in the period after 1949 because and to the extent that they were actually consistent with traditional Chinese values, "we could not accept seminars (classroom discussion), a widely adopted teaching method in Western universities, as an effective way of enhancing a student's independent thinking."[17] And while China's "transformation towards a market economy . . . prompted reforms in the classrooms," including even the use of seminars,[18] my own experience in Tianjin reinforces the prevailing stereotype in which students seem to prefer the traditional lecture format rather than the seminar-discussion format I had originally intended. Faced with a largely unresponsive class, and without the benefit of a seminar-friendly classroom setting (i.e., with chairs set in rows in front of a lectern instead of chairs deployed around a large table), I take the path of least resistance and do most of the talking myself. Still, I begin to wonder if at least part of the reticence of my Chinese students to speak out in class is due to their insecurities with spoken English, rather than to a culturally specific aversion to the expression of individuality within a group context.

However, my one-on-one interaction with students in an architectural design studio context is more productive: perhaps this is because "Chinese teachers assume the role of mentor and role model far more so than Western teachers."[19] In other words, the more informal (and personal) type of academic interaction that occurs in the design studio, where the instructor assumes the role of a mentor, seems to work out better than the seminar format, where a student's individuality may be viewed as a threat to the "solidarity" of the group or where a student's questioning may be viewed as a challenge to the authority of the teacher.

The role of English in Chinese education, however, has another dimension altogether, which brings up my second example of soft infrastructure in relation to traditional Chinese culture. Some scholars situate English instruction within a "discourse of linguistic instrumentalism, which emphasizes utilitarianism of learning English for sustaining economic development of a society and for social mobility as individuals."[20] My own experience in Tianjin appears to challenge this instrumentalist view, as I am initially asked to teach a cohort of visiting *international* students rather than the Chinese architectural students whose exposure to English-language coursework would presumably not only benefit themselves but also advance China's "economic competitiveness in the global market."[21] Be this as it may, the Fulbright staff in Beijing is not at all happy about my proposed teaching assignment and intervenes, insisting that the *American* interest in funding me as a Fulbright scholar requires that I interact primarily with Chinese students. It amuses me to think that I am simultaneously considered a tool of both Chinese and American foreign policy objectives, while I naively embark on this Fulbright adventure as if it is in *my* interest! Ultimately, a compromise is reached in which the number of international students in my classes is limited to about 10% of the total enrollment.

Overall, my personal experience as a Fulbright scholar is mostly positive, and my engagement with cross-cultural analysis will be extremely valuable as I refine and reconsider my own teaching and writing after returning home. I leave China knowing that the mix of traditional and contemporary cultural practices I have experienced in Tianjin, embedded within increasingly state-of-the-art infrastructural elements (both *hard* and *soft*), is not likely to survive in its current form as modernization and urbanization move forward with incredible speed. And I can't help but be aware that the basis for the proliferation of cheap goods and cheap transportation is the widening income gap between China's capitalist elites and the agricultural, factory, and service workers, who still struggle with low wages, long hours, disruption of family cohesion, and unhealthful environmental conditions. This remains true despite the well-known fact that "as many as six hundred million people in China have climbed out of poverty" since 1981 and have seen their economic conditions improve.[22]

Getting even a glimpse of this rapid development of infrastructural elements—and the cultural practices they support—has been, for me, the most compelling aspect of my five months in Tianjin. In other words, the point of teaching in China was not to return to the US having drawn any profound conclusions about the nature and result of China's rapid urban expansion, which is, in any case, a work in progress. Rather, what was most interesting to me was the opportunity to sense and engage the unprecedented transformation of a society at a time when so many messy artifacts of its transformation are still visible and exposed.

Notes

1. Jon Lang and Walter Moleski, *Functionalism Revisited: Architectural Theory and Practice and the Behavioral Sciences* (Surrey, England, and Burlington, VT: Ashgate Publishing, Ltd., 2010), 117. Print.
2. Henry Zhang and David Brown, "Understanding Urban Residential Water Use in Beijing and Tianjin, China," *Habitat International* 29 (2005): 469–491. Print.

3. "Demolition of Tianjin's Old City," *Bricoleurbanism*, April 12, 2010. Web. 14 November 2018.
4. Thomas Campanella, *The Concrete Dragon* (New York: Princeton Architectural Press, 2008), 179. Print.
5. Lauri Paltema, "Tangshan Earthquake, 1976," *DisasterHistory*, n.d. Web. 05 June 2018.
6. Lorin Yochim, "Navigating the Aspirational City: Processes of Accumulation in China's Socialist Market Economy," in *Spotlight on China: Changes in Education under China's Market Economy*, ed. Shibao Guo and Yan Guo (Rotterdam, Netherlands: Sense Publishers, 2016), 354. Print.
7. Campanella, 149.
8. Xin Guo and Frank Gallo, *Multinational Companies in China: Navigating the Eight Common Management Pitfalls in China* (Bingley, UK: Emerald Publishing Limited, 2017). Print.
9. Farhad Manjoo, "Even Uber Couldn't Bridge the China Divide," *New York Times*, August 1, 2016. Web. 14 November 2018.
10. Ibid.
11. Peter Cai, *Understanding China's Belt and Road Initiative* (Sydney: Lowy Institute for International Policy, 2017).
12. "40 Years Ago, the Tangshan Earthquake Hit Tianjin, Tangshan City, 64% Houses Were Destroyed," *BestChinaNews*, July 28, 2016. Web. 14 November 2018.
13. An Yin, Xiangjiang Yu, and Jing Liu-Zeng, "A Possible Seismic Gap and High Earthquake Hazard in the North China Basin," *Geology* 43, no. 1 (2015): 19–22. Print.
14. Jerome McKinney, *Budgeting for Sustainability: An Approach for American Policy-Making* (Jefferson, NC: McFarland, 2017), 67. Print.
15. Wing-Wah Law, "Social Change, Citizenship, and Citizenship Education in China Since the Late 1970," in *Spotlight on China: Changes in Education under China's Market Economy*, ed. Shibao Guo and Yan Guo (Rotterdam, Netherlands: Sense Publishers, 2016), 39. Print.
16. Ken Levinson, "Cultural Differences and Learning Styles of Chinese and European Trades Students," *Institute for Learning Styles Journal* 1 (Fall 2007). Print.
17. Gu Mingyuan, *Cultural Foundations of Chinese Education* (Leiden, Netherlands: Brill, 2014), 216. Print.
18. Lei Zhang, Ruyue Dai, and Kai Yu, "Chinese Higher Education since 1977: Possibilities, Challenges and Tensions," in *Spotlight on China: Changes in Education under China's Market Economy*, ed. Shibao Guo and Yan Guo (Rotterdam, Netherlands: Sense Publishers, 2016), 182. Print.
19. Levinson, 13.
20. Yan Guo, "The Impact of the Market Economy on English Teachers," in *Spotlight on China: Changes in Education under China's Market Economy*, ed. Shibao Guo and Yan Guo (Rotterdam, Netherlands: Sense Publishers, 2016), 119. Print.
21. Ibid.
22. Cynthia Estlund, *A New Deal for China's Workers?* (Cambridge, MA: Harvard University Press, 2017), 2. Print.

Contributors

Jesse Butler is Associate Professor in the Department of Philosophy and Religion at the University of Central Arkansas, USA, where he teaches courses in the philosophy of mind, critical thinking, philosophy of language, and philosophy for living. His research focuses on theories of self-knowledge, with his book *Rethinking Introspection* (Palgrave Macmillan, 2013) offering a pluralist and naturalistic approach to understanding the first-person perspective. Dr. Butler was also a US Fulbright Scholar during the 2016–2017 academic year, teaching courses on cross-cultural approaches to self-knowledge at Jinan University in Guangzhou, China. His current research involves the application of theories of self and mind to issues in the philosophy of psychiatry and environmental philosophy, towards the end of cultivating human well-being and sustainability through understanding the interconnected plurality of our embodied existence in the world.

Amy Cheng was born in Taiwan, and grew up in Brazil, Oklahoma, and Texas. She received a BFA in painting from the University of Texas at Austin and an MFA from Hunter College, City University of New York. She is Professor in the Art Department at the State University of New York at New Paltz, USA. She has also taught at Bard College, Princeton University, and Hunter College. She has a dual career in public art and studio painting. She has installed numerous public art commissions including at the Seattle-Tacoma International Airport, the Lambert-St. Louis Airport, the Jacksonville Airport, at transportation hubs such as New York City subway stations, a Chicago El station, and the Valley Regional Bus Terminal in Boise, Idaho. Her paintings are in various collections including the New York University Langone Medical Center, Hewlett-Packard, Novartis Pharmaceuticals, Wyeth Pharmaceuticals, Chevron Corporation, and The Hyde Collection.

Jeannette W. Cockroft, co-editor, is Associate Professor of History and Political Science at Schreiner University in Kerrville, Texas, USA. She has a BA in East Asian languages and culture from the University of Pennsylvania; an MA in political science from the University of Kansas; and a PhD in history from Texas A&M University. Her research on Margaret Chase Smith has appeared in *Maine History*, the *Washington Post*, and *Women in the American Political System: An Encyclopedia of Women as Voters, Candidates, and Officeholders*. During the 2016–2017 academic year, she lectured on American culture and politics as well as the 2016 US presidential election in both China and Mongolia.

Michael Fetters, MD, MPH, MA, is Professor of Family Medicine, University of Michigan, USA, and Adjunct Professor, Peking University Health Science Center, China. He earned his BA (Japanese studies) and MD degree from The Ohio State University. He completed his residency training (family medicine), research fellowship (Robert Wood Johnson Clinical Scholars Program—health services research), and MPH (clinical epidemiology) at the University of North Carolina, Chapel Hill. He earned an MA (medical anthropology and ethics) from Michigan State University. He founded and directs the Japanese Family Health Program (https://medicine.umich.edu/dept/japanese-family-health-program), a clinical program providing culturally and linguistically sensitive care, celebrating 25 years of service in 2019. In 2016, as Fulbright Distinguished Chair in the Social Sciences, he taught the first mixed methods research graduate course in China.He co-founded and co-directs the University of Michigan Mixed Methods Program (https://www.mixed methods.org), a think tank on mixed methods research. He serves as co-chief editor of the *Journal of Mixed Methods Research.*

Shin Freedman, co-editor, is Head of Scholarly Resources & Collections of Whittemore Library at Framingham State University in Massachusetts, USA. She has an MBA from Bentley University, and an MLS from Simmons University, Graduate School of Library and Information Science, Boston, and a BA from the Catholic University of Taegu, Korea. In 2016, she received a Fulbright US Lecturer Award to China and taught graduate courses at Zhejiang University in Hangzhou, China. In 2015, she was appointed as a founding member of the editorial board of *Charleston Insights in Library, Archival, and Information Science* in Charleston, South Carolina. Her research interests include academic library leadership, collegiality, mentorship, and bullying in higher education. Her publications include a book, *Becoming a Library Leader* (2019). Her research has been published in leading library and information science journals. Additionally, she has won literary awards around the world, including the Shanghai International Writing and Recitation Contest, the Vermont Writer in Action Award, and the Korean-American Non-Fiction Literary Competition Award.

Tim Maciel's academic and professional interests have focused on international/intercultural education, higher education administration, and language education. He holds an EdD from Harvard University, USA, in administration, planning, and social policy, an MA from Harvard in international education, an MAT from the School for International Training, and a BA from Gonzaga University. In addition to his Fulbright experience, his 12-plus years of experience overseas includes two tours in South Korea as a Peace Corps volunteer, and nearly four years with the International Catholic Migration Commission serving Southeast Asian refugees in the Philippines. In the US, he has served as a senior college administrator in several private and public institutions and is currently founder/director of Educational Solutions of New England, consulting on internationalization strategies in higher education and faculty development. He and his wife, Kathleen Maceda, reside in Vermont and are proud parents of a son, Charles, and daughter, Sarah.

Pat Munday (PhD, Cornell University, 1990), co-editor, is Professor of Science and Technology Studies at Montana Tech in Butte, Montana, USA. His teaching and research include the history of science, American society and technology, semiotics, and environmental studies. His publications range from the history of German chemistry to a social history of Montana's Big Hole River, and his work has appeared in the *British Journal for the History of Science, Technology & Culture*, and other journals. He is in his third term as president of the Mai Wah Society, a non-profit that operates a Chinese museum of history and culture. He has raised approximately $1.5 million from grant writing for various projects, including "bricks and mortar" work on the Mai Wah Museum and stream restoration for native fish. He has held three Fulbright awards: one as a graduate researcher in West Germany (1987–1988); one as a visiting scholar with Southwest University in Chongqing, China (2012); and one as a visiting scholar with Ningxia University in Yinchuan, China (2017).

Mary Ni received her BS in psychology from Springfield College, USA, her MEd in counseling psychology from Boston College, and her EdD in counseling and consulting psychology from Harvard University. She has worked as a psychologist, guidance counselor, university dean, and director of multicultural education. Currently she teaches emotional literacy and other education courses at Salem State University in Salem,

Massachusetts. A major interest of hers is to "give psychology away" to people who are not psychologists or counselors but who would benefit from understanding and using psychological information in their professional and personal lives. She includes everyone in this category. Two examples of her writing can be found in *Sextant*, the Salem State University Journal: "Speaking the Unspeakable," *Sextant*. Fall 2012, Volume XX, No. 1; and "Opening Circles: A Simple Way to Begin to Build Interactive Classroom Communities," *Sextant*. Spring 2006, Volume XIV, No. 1.

Jonathan Ochshorn is a registered architect with an academic background in structural engineering and urban design as well as architecture. Prior to joining the faculty at Cornell University, USA, in 1988, he taught at City College of New York while serving as Associate Director of the City College Architectural Center, a research center supplying technical assistance to community groups in New York City. Since 1976, he has also practiced architecture and urban design in New York and California. His publications include studies on energy loss through tapered insulation, as well as the political and economic underpinnings of sustainable building. He is the author of two editions of the textbook *Structural Elements for Architects and Builders*, and has developed several interactive computer programs, many of which are available online at no cost. Professor Ochshorn teaches courses in construction technology, structures, and the politics of sustainable design.

Index